I0759488

LAROUSSE FRENCH COOKING

LAROUSSE FRENCH COOKING

The definitive collection of classic recipes from the French home kitchen

Contents

The North

and the Paris Basin

Flemish-style Asparagus

ASPERGES À LA FLAMANDE

Serves 4

Preparation time: 15 mins

Cooking time: 20–25 mins

Ingredients

1.6kg (3lb 8oz) white asparagus spears

6 hard-boiled eggs

200g (7oz) butter

4 tablespoons finely chopped parsley

salt and freshly ground black pepper

White asparagus is grown in the same way as green asparagus but the spears are picked while they are still underground and so, deprived of sunlight, they do not develop chlorophyll to turn them green. White asparagus is sweeter and more tender than the green variety.

1 Line up the asparagus spears side by side on a board and trim the ends so that the spears are of equal length. Using a vegetable peeler, peel each spear from the tip to its end, then rinse the spears under cold running water without letting them soak. Tie them into small bundles with kitchen string.

2 Stand the bundles upright in a tall saucepan of salted boiling water with the stems in the water and the tips above, cover the pan with a tight-fitting lid and cook for 20–25 minutes, depending on the thickness of the spears and how fresh they are, until tender. Drain, place on a plate covered with a clean tea towel and leave the spears to cool very slightly.

3 Meanwhile, shell the eggs and cut them lengthways in half. Separate the yolks from the whites and chop both finely, keeping them separate. Melt the butter over a low heat and pour it into a very hot jar or similar heatproof container.

4 Serve the asparagus while still hot, with the chopped egg whites and yolks and the melted butter and chopped parsley separately alongside. Let diners prepare and season the butter sauce according to personal taste, crushing their preferred amounts of hard-boiled yolks and whites and mixing with the butter and parsley before spooning the sauce over the asparagus or dipping the spears into it.

Maroilles Cheese Tart

TARTE AU MAROILLES

Serves 4	Preparation time: 15 mins	Resting time: 1 hour	Cooking time: 20–25 mins

Ingredients

10g (¼oz) fresh yeast (or half a 7g/¼oz sachet fast-action dried yeast)

150ml (5fl oz) warm milk

200g (7oz) plain flour

1 egg

40g (1½oz) butter, melted, plus extra for greasing

pinch of salt

¼ Maroilles cheese (180g/6¼oz), sliced

freshly ground black pepper

Maroilles is a soft cows' milk cheese from northern France that is said to have been invented in the 10th century by a monk of the same name. It is cream-coloured with a soft, orange, washed rind, a very strong smell but with a deceptively mild taste, becoming stronger as it ages. Sold in small rectangular blocks, it is usually available only from specialist cheese shops or suppliers, but Reblochon, Pont l'Évêque or Chaumes could be used instead.

1 First make the dough for the tart case. If using fresh yeast, dissolve it in the warm milk.

2 Sift the flour into a mixing bowl (then stir in the dried yeast, if using). Make a well in the centre and add the egg, melted butter, dissolved fresh yeast (if using) and milk and the salt.

3 Using a balloon whisk, mix the flour with the other ingredients until you have a smooth, sticky dough.

4 Grease a 26cm (10½-inch) flan tin with butter and tip in the dough, spreading it out a little using a spatula.

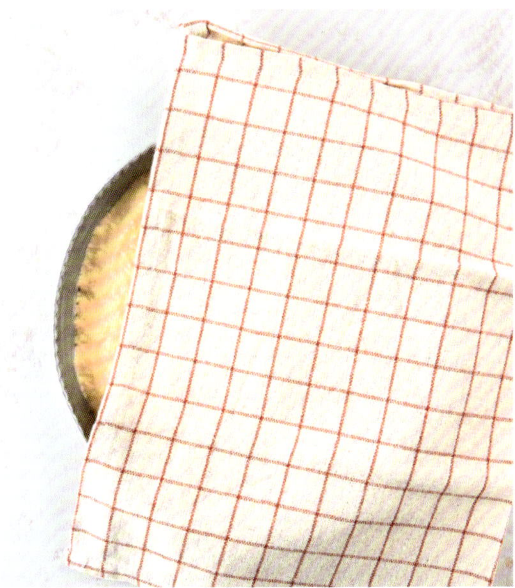

5 Cover with a clean tea towel and leave the dough to rise at room temperature for 1 hour until it has increased in volume.

6 Preheat the oven to 200°C (400°F), Gas Mark 6. When the dough is well risen, lay the cheese slices on top and season with pepper. Bake for 20–25 minutes. Serve the tart warm with a green salad.

Grilled Bloaters with Potato Salad

BOUFFIS GRILLÉS, POMMES À L'HUILE

Serves 4

Preparation time: 15 mins

Soaking time: 3–4 hours

Cooking time: 30–35 mins

Ingredients

4 very thick, light-coloured bloater (smoked herring) fillets

milk, for soaking

500g (1lb 2oz) small waxy new potatoes

1 onion, chopped

1 tablespoon hot mustard

1 teaspoon lemon juice

2 tablespoons olive oil

1 bunch of parsley, chopped

salt

A *bouffi* is the Upper Normandy equivalent of a bloater, or smoked herring. The herring is first cured by lightly salting and then smoked whole until it is straw-coloured.

1. Place the bloaters side by side in a shallow dish, pour over enough milk to cover them and leave them to soak for 3–4 hours.
2. Wash the potatoes thoroughly, wipe with kitchen paper and steam for 20 minutes or until cooked through.
3. Meanwhile, season the onion with salt, then mix with the mustard and lemon juice in a large bowl. Leave to stand for a few minutes so that the onion begins to soften.
4. Preheat the oven grill. Once the potatoes are cooked, remove them from the steamer. Peel off their skins while they are still warm and cut into thick slices. Toss the potato slices in the oil along with the chopped parsley, then add to the onion and mustard mixture. Keep warm.
5. Drain and pat the bloaters dry. Grill them on the middle shelf of the oven for 10–12 minutes, depending on how thick they are, until cooked, turning them over halfway through.
6. Pile the still-warm potatoes into a serving dish. Cut the grilled bloaters into 1cm (½-inch) chunks and add to the potatoes. Mix and serve immediately.

Flemish Beef Carbonnade

CARBONADE FLAMANDE

Serves 6 | **Preparation time: 20 mins** | **Cooking time: 3 hours 20 mins**

Ingredients

1.5kg (3lb 5oz) braising steak (chuck), cut into large pieces

100g (3½oz) lard

300g (10½oz) onions, chopped

3 tablespoons plain flour

3 tablespoons brown sugar

3 tablespoons red wine vinegar

1 bay leaf

1 hop cone (if available)

1 litre (1¾ pints) Flemish blonde ale *(bière de garde blonde)*

3 large slices of *pain d'épices* (French spice bread)

2 tablespoons hot mustard

salt and freshly ground black pepper

Hop cones are the flowers of the hop plant and they add the characteristic flavour, aroma and bitterness to beer. They can be bought online from home-brewing websites. *Bière de garde*, which translates as 'beer for keeping', is a strong pale ale that is traditionally brewed in Nord-Pas-de-Calais.

1 Season the pieces of beef with salt and pepper. Melt half the lard in a cast-iron casserole and sauté the beef in batches over a high heat for 1–2 minutes on each side. Remove to a plate and set aside.

2 Pour off any fat remaining in the casserole or remove with a spoon, return the casserole to a low heat and add the remaining lard. Add the onions and fry gently for 10–12 minutes until they are soft and melting. Stir in the flour and sugar and cook, stirring continuously, for 1 minute, then pour in the vinegar and mix it in. Remove the onions with a slotted spoon and set them aside.

3 Preheat the oven to 150°C (300°F), Gas Mark 2. Layer the onions and beef alternately in the casserole, add the bay leaf and tuck the hop cone (if you have one) in the centre. Season with salt and pepper and pour in the juices from the beef and the beer, which should cover the meat.

4 Spread both sides of the *pain d'épices* slices with the mustard and lay the slices on top. Cover the casserole, placing crumpled foil around the bottom edge of the lid so that the pan is tightly sealed. Cook in the oven for 3 hours.

Tip

A classic brasserie dish, carbonnade is usually served with mashed potatoes or chips. In northern France, the traditional drink to accompany it would be a powerful brown or red *gueuze* (lambic) beer, or a fruity, well-rounded red wine from the Rhône Valley.

Potted Meat

POTJEVLEESH

Serves 10

Preparation time: 20 mins

Marinating time: 24 hours

Chilling time: 12 hours

Cooking time: 3½ hours

Ingredients

800g (1lb 12oz) veal neck or shoulder on the bone

4 rabbit saddles

800g (1lb 12oz) pork shoulder on the bone

4 cloves

6 bay leaves

6 garlic cloves, peeled

1 celery stick, cut into short lengths

2 litres (3½ pints) white beer

20 juniper berries

500g (1lb 2oz) onions, chopped

2 carrots, sliced into rounds

3 thyme sprigs

45ml (3 tablespoons) Genièvre de Houlle (or an artisanal gin)

330ml (11½fl oz) distilled white vinegar

40g (1½oz) plain flour

1 tablespoon cold water

salt and freshly ground black pepper

Another French-Flemish dish, made by slowly cooking several different meats together in a terrine dish in a low oven, the pieces of meat being held together by the natural gelatine they release.

1. The day before you want to cook the potted meat, chop the veal, rabbit and pork into large pieces, without removing the bones. Put the meats, cloves, 4 of the bay leaves, the garlic and celery in a large bowl. Pour over the beer to cover and leave to marinate for 24 hours in the refrigerator.

2. The next day, preheat the oven to 150°C (300°F), Gas Mark 2. Drain the meats, reserving the marinade, and layer them alternately with the juniper berries in an ovenproof terrine dish, packing them down well. Cover with the onions and carrots, season with salt and pepper and lay the thyme sprigs and remaining 2 bay leaves on top.

3. Strain the marinade into a saucepan, add the Genièvre de Houlle (or gin) and vinegar and heat until warm. Pour enough of the liquid into the terrine dish to cover the meat.

4. Make a soft dough by mixing the flour with the cold water. Roll the dough into a long sausage and press it around the edge of the terrine dish so that when the lid is placed on top and pressed down, it sinks into the dough and the terrine dish is tightly sealed.

5. Lift the terrine into a deep baking tin or deep ovenproof dish containing enough water to come two-thirds of the way up the sides of the terrine. Cook in the oven for 3½ hours.

6. Remove the terrine from its bain-marie and leave to cool. Refrigerate for at least 12 hours before serving the potted meat cold.

Tip

Both the French and English names for this dish mean literally 'meat in a pot', and because it requires several different kinds of meat, you cannot make it in small quantities. It is a summer dish, so ideal for when you have lots of guests to entertain, as it's simple to make and can be prepared in advance. Serve it with salad or chips and a selection of condiments such as pickles, mustard, mayonnaise or others of your choice.

Chicken Waterzoï

WATERZOÏ DE POULET

Serves 4–6

Preparation time: 15 mins

Cooking time: 1 hour 25 mins

Ingredients

1 litre (1¾ pints) chicken stock

1 chicken, weighing 1.5–1.7kg (3lb 5oz–3lb 12oz)

80g (3oz) butter, plus extra for spreading on the toast

5 parsley sprigs, plus extra, chopped, to garnish

white parts of 5 leeks, trimmed, cleaned and finely chopped

2 celery sticks, finely chopped

3 onions, chopped

2 egg yolks

250ml (9fl oz) crème fraîche

juice of 1 lemon

6–8 slices of bread, toasted

salt and freshly ground black pepper

Originally a creamy fish stew, this recipe works equally well made with chicken.

1 Heat the stock in a large saucepan, add the chicken, making sure it is immersed in the stock, and simmer gently for 30 minutes.

2 Meanwhile, melt the butter in a flameproof casserole with the parsley sprigs, add the leeks, celery and onions and cook over a low heat for 20 minutes. Season with salt and pepper.

3 Drain the chicken from the stock, reserving the stock, and cut the chicken into 8 pieces, removing as many of the bones as possible. Place the chicken pieces in the casserole on top of the vegetables. Pour in enough of the stock to cover the chicken and simmer for another 30 minutes.

4 Drain the chicken pieces from the casserole. Whisk the egg yolks with the crème fraîche, add the lemon juice, then pour into the casserole. Stir over a low heat for 5 minutes, without letting the sauce boil. Check for seasoning, adding more if necessary. Return the chicken pieces to the casserole.

5 Serve directly from the casserole, garnished with chopped parsley and accompanied with the toasted bread, spread with butter.

Chicken in Beer

COQ À LA BIÈRE

Serves 6

Preparation time: 1 hour

Cooking time: 2 hours

Ingredients

1 chicken, weighing about 2kg (4lb 8oz), with its liver

1 lightly salted lean bacon rasher, rinded

20g (¾oz) lard

2 tablespoons gin

1 tablespoon plain flour

1 litre (1¾ pints) blonde beer

100g (3½oz) shallots, finely sliced or chopped

2 garlic cloves, finely sliced or chopped

1 bouquet garni

24 small pearl onions, peeled and halved lengthways

50g (1¾oz) butter

250g (9oz) small button mushrooms, trimmed and sliced

juice of ½ lemon

150ml (5fl oz) crème fraîche (optional)

salt and freshly ground black pepper

***Coq au vin* is a classic French dish but cooks in the north of France prefer to use local blonde beer instead of wine, as it adds a distinctly malty flavour and gives the sauce a rich colour.**

1 Cut the chicken into joints, chop the chicken liver and set both aside.

2 Put the bacon rasher in a saucepan, cover with cold water and bring to the boil. Drain and then cut or snip the bacon into small lardons. Preheat the oven to 150°C (300°F), Gas Mark 2.

3 Heat the lard in a flameproof casserole over a low heat and brown the bacon pieces. Remove them with a slotted spoon and set aside. Increase the heat, add the chicken joints to the casserole and fry them until they are evenly golden all over, turning the pieces several times and removing them from the casserole once they are sufficiently coloured.

4 Drain the fat from the casserole and return the chicken joints to it. Add the gin, bring to the boil and flambé (set alight briefly). Dust with the flour and add the beer, pouring it in slowly and gradually to avoid it foaming. Add the shallots, garlic and bouquet garni and season with salt and pepper. Cover the casserole, making a tight seal between the pot and the lid with a flour and water dough (see page 18) or by placing crumpled foil around the bottom edge of the lid. Cook in the oven for 1½ hours.

5 Meanwhile, in a frying pan, fry the pearl onions in the butter for 20 minutes over a very low heat, stirring frequently until they are meltingly soft. Add the mushrooms and lemon juice, cover the pan and leave to cook for 10 minutes.

6 Remove the casserole from the oven, lift out the chicken joints with a slotted spoon and place them in a shallow dish. Keep warm. Remove the bouquet garni and add the cooking juices from the pearl onions and mushrooms. Boil over a high heat to reduce the liquid by half, then add the pearl onions and mushrooms and stir or whisk in the crème fraîche (if using). Pour the sauce over the chicken and serve.

SOMETHING TO DRINK
WITH THAT?

Speciality Beers

A world away from the light blonde beers that are frequently found on sale these days, brewers in northern France have long produced dark malt-based high-fermentation beers using the classic British method of infusion – or what are known as 'speciality beers'. At the end of the 19th century, this traditional method of brewing gradually gave way to producing low-fermentation beers that were developed in Germany and called 'lagers'. However, since 1950, beers produced traditionally have slowly not just made a comeback but also become quite trendy. Today, several French brewers, especially in the north, sell specific products that have pronounced flavours, such as Jenlain, Pelforth brown and 3 Monts.

Some Like It Dry, Some Like It Sweet

The jewel in the crown of the Normandy and Brittany regions, cider has it all! Whether it is sweet, semi-sweet, semi-dry or dry, cider will never attack your taste buds (nor your head) thanks to its low level of alcohol and its tiny refreshing bubbles. Made from apple juice, it is traditionally drunk on feast days such as Candlemas or Epiphany and is the go-to drink in creperies, where you will always be offered a small glass of cider to accompany your galette or crepe. The ciders of Brittany and Normandy also benefit from being granted IGP (Protected Geographical Indication) status. It is, of course, also made far beyond the borders of France, notably in Canada, Germany and the UK.

A Drop of Calva?

Calvados, often served as a digestive, is a brandy produced by distilling Normandy cider. It is then aged in oak barrels and graded according to its age and how it is produced, whether industrially in a factory or on a farm. These grades are fine *(fine)*, old *(vieux)*, old reserve *(vieille réserve)* or beyond age *(hors d'âge)*. Calvados has never lost its popularity and remains one of Normandy's most emblematic specialities, with the majority of farms producing their own version of this powerful alcohol. It is both served as a drink and used as an ingredient in the local cuisine.

Who Could Forget the Famous Little Bubbles!

Let's raise our glass to the most celebrated French alcoholic drink of all – champagne! Synonymous with luxury and an incomparable product, its tiny bubbles have conquered the world, beginning with France, which has made it one of its emblematic historical and gastronomic icons. The techniques for making champagne and its production area are recognized with AOC (Controlled Designation of Origin) status, which prohibits any other sparkling wine produced outside the Champagne vineyards from calling itself 'champagne'. It has remained an exclusively French product since its first appearance at the end of the 17th century and its fame is such that it has even been designated a UNESCO World Heritage Site since 2015. Cheers and *tchin-tchin!*

Crème de Cassis, Queen of the Kir!

Everyone loves a Kir. The invention of this delicious cocktail, which mixes white wine or champagne with the blackcurrant liqueur *crème de cassis*, has proved a launch pad for the latter's production. Intensely aromatic, *crème de cassis* is made by macerating blackcurrants in alcohol, to which sugar is then added. It has been a speciality of Dijon and the Côte d'Or of Burgundy since the early 1840s and is drunk mainly in cocktails, such as the famous Kir or the *mêlé-cass*, made by mixing one-third *crème de cassis* with two-thirds *marc*, a spirit distilled from the liquor produced from the skins and stalks of grapes after they have been pressed to make wine.

Anyone for a 'Petit Jaune'?

Contrary to what one might think, the region of France where the most pastis is drunk is not in the south but in Hauts-de-France, between Calais and Paris. Nicknamed the 'little yellow one' due to the colour pastis turns when water is added to it, this aniseed-flavoured spirit, traditionally produced in the Marseille region, has become a national institution. Today, the Pernod Ricard company, the result of a merger between two former competitors, dominates the market with the two best-selling brands, Ricard and 51. However, other less well-known but equally high-quality brands include Casanis, Henri Bardouin and Janot. Pastis is traditionally drunk as an aperitif, diluted with cold water and served on the rocks. There are also pastis cocktails using syrup, such as Perroquet with mint syrup, Tomate with grenadine syrup and the famous Mauresque, which is made with orgeat syrup. However, do remember to measure the correct proportions to avoid 'drowning' your drink and risk ending up with a *flanby* (a type of crème caramel once popular with children), as they say in the city of Marseille.

All Roads Lead to Rum!

Made from sugar cane, traditional molasses rum (known as *sucrerie)* has been a speciality of the island of Réunion for several centuries. In the 17th century, sugar cane began to be grown on the island in plantations and its distilled juice (known as *vesou)* made it possible to produce rum. Two centuries later, the growth of industrialization led to an increase in sugar production and rum was then obtained from cane molasses, the syrupy residue that results from the crystallization of sugar. Called tafia, this rum is less fine but continues to be made on Réunion.

Chicory and Ham Gratin

ENDIVES AU JAMBON

Serves 4

Preparation time: 30 mins

Cooking time: 30 mins

Ingredients

4 very white, firm heads of chicory

90g (3¼oz) butter, plus extra for greasing

30g (1oz) plain flour

500ml (18fl oz) milk

large pinch of freshly grated nutmeg

60g (2¼oz) hard cheese, such as Gruyère or Cheddar, grated

4 slices of cooked ham

salt and freshly ground black pepper

The salty ham and rich cheese sauce make the perfect foil for the slightly bitter flavour of the chicory. In France, Gruyère would most likely be used to make the sauce, but a strong Cheddar also works well.

1 Remove any damaged outer leaves from the chicory and cut out the core.

2 Heat 30g (1oz) of the butter in a frying pan over a gentle heat, add the chicory heads, cover with a lid and leave to cook in their own juices until just tender.

3 Meanwhile, melt another 30g (1oz) of the butter in a saucepan, then take the pan off the heat, add the flour and stir until smooth. Return the pan to the heat and cook for 2 minutes without letting the butter and flour roux colour. Remove the pan from the heat again and gradually pour in all the milk, whisking continuously to prevent any lumps forming. Return the pan to the heat once more and cook the sauce for 10–12 minutes, stirring continuously to begin with until it thickens, and then stirring from time to time to prevent the sauce sticking on the bottom of the pan. Season with salt, pepper and the nutmeg and stir in half the grated cheese, mixing well.

4 Preheat the oven to its highest setting. Grease a gratin dish or baking tin with butter. Drain the chicory and wrap each head in a slice of ham. Place the rolls side by side in the dish, then spoon over the cheese sauce until the rolls are coated.

5 Sprinkle the rest of the grated cheese on top. Cut the remaining butter into small pieces and dot over the chicory. Bake for 15 minutes or until golden brown on top. Serve immediately.

Grilled Andouillettes with Fried Onions

ANDOUILLETTES GRILLÉES AUX OIGNONS FRITS

Serves 4 | **Preparation time: 15 mins** | **Cooking time: 15 mins**

Ingredients

4 large onions
beer, for coating
plain flour, for coating
4 andouillettes
oil, for deep-frying
salt and freshly ground black pepper

Andouillettes are very popular with the French but rarely eaten (or sold) outside of France. The most likely reason for these rustic sausages never having gained universal appeal is not just their coarse texture and strong smell but the fact that they are made from pork intestines!

1 Slice the onions widthways into rounds, keeping the rings in place. Pour beer into a shallow dish and some flour into a separate dish. Season the flour with salt and pepper, mixing well.

2 Preheat an oven grill or barbecue. Prick each andouillette 2 or 3 times with the tip of a small, sharp knife. Grill for about 10 minutes under the oven grill or directly on a barbecue, turning the andouillettes several times, until they are golden all over.

3 Meanwhile, heat oil for deep-frying in a large pan to 180°C (350°F). Dip the onion rounds one at a time in the beer and then in the flour until they are coated. Lower the rounds, a few at a time, into the hot oil and fry until golden brown. Remove them from the oil with a slotted spoon or skimmer and drain on kitchen paper.

4 Transfer the andouillettes to a hot serving dish and surround them with the fried onion rounds. Serve while still hot, with a beer.

Ham and Cheese Crepes

FICELLES PICARDES

Serves 4

Preparation time: 15 mins

Cooking time: 25 mins

Ingredients

50g (1¾oz) butter, plus extra for greasing

2 shallots, finely sliced or chopped

400g (14oz) button mushrooms, trimmed and thickly sliced

4 savoury crepes

4 slices of cooked ham

8 tablespoons crème fraîche

100g (3½oz) Emmental cheese, grated

salt and freshly ground black pepper

The French name for this dish translates as 'Picardy string' and is a typical example of the regional cuisine, said to have been created in 1950 by a chef in Amiens for local dignitaries who were attending an exhibition in the city. The filled crepes can be served as a starter or as a main course accompanied with a crisp green salad dressed with walnut vinegar, and a light beer.

1. Grease a gratin dish or baking tin with butter.

2. Preheat the oven to 220°C (425°F), Gas Mark 7. Heat the butter in a saucepan and gently sauté the shallots until they are translucent. Add the mushrooms and leave them to cook, uncovered, for 10 minutes until they release their liquid.

3. Place one crepe in the gratin dish. Remove any rind from the ham and cover the crepe with one slice. Add one-quarter of the mushroom mixture and coat with 1 tablespoon of crème fraîche. Season with salt and pepper and roll up the crepe. Repeat with the 3 remaining crepes, laying the rolls side by side in the gratin dish. Spoon the rest of the crème fraîche over the rolls and sprinkle generously with the grated cheese. Bake for 10 minutes or until the cheese topping has browned. Serve immediately.

Steak with Shallots

PIÈCES DE BOEUF AUX ÉCHALOTES

Serves 4

Preparation time: 20 mins

Cooking time: 45 mins

Ingredients

16 small shallots, peeled

200ml (7fl oz) sunflower oil

1 carrot, cut into small dice

1 small celery stick (about 30g/1oz), finely sliced

1 bottle red wine

1 tablespoon brown sugar

25g (1oz) butter, cut into small pieces

4 rump steaks, at room temperature

salt and freshly ground black pepper

chopped parsley, to garnish

If you see *pièce de boeuf* on a French menu, it means you will be served a good-quality steak, but the cut will depend on what the chef has chosen to cook that day. For this recipe, a tender cut is needed, so rump steak works particularly well.

1. Put the shallots in a saucepan and pour over enough of the oil to cover them. Season with salt and pepper. Heat the oil until hot, then leave the shallots to cook over a very gentle heat for 30 minutes. They must be a soft, almost melting consistency but not golden. Leave the shallots to cool in the oil before draining them in a sieve.
2. Put the carrot and celery in another saucepan, then add the wine and bubble over a high heat to reduce it by two-thirds. Add the sugar and leave to cook for a few more minutes until you have a sauce with a syrupy consistency.
3. Take the pan off the heat and gradually whisk in the butter. Add the drained shallots to the sauce and keep hot.
4. Heat 1 tablespoon of oil in a frying pan and fry the rump steaks over a medium heat for 3–4 minutes on each side. Season with salt and pepper.
5. Serve the steaks immediately with the shallot sauce, accompanied with mashed Jerusalem artichokes or celeriac and garnished with chopped parsley.

Navarin of Lamb

NAVARIN D'AGNEAU

Serves 4–6

Preparation time: 25 mins

Cooking time: 1 hour

Ingredients

600g (1lb 5oz) boneless shoulder of lamb

600g (1lb 5oz) boneless neck of lamb

2 tomatoes

2 tablespoons groundnut oil

1 tablespoon plain flour

freshly grated nutmeg

2 garlic gloves, chopped

1 bouquet garni

2 bunches of new-season carrots

200g (7oz) baby turnips

1 bunch of baby onions, peeled

300g (10½oz) green beans, trimmed and halved lengthways

300g (10½oz) fresh peas in their pods, shelled

25g (1oz) butter

salt and freshly ground black pepper

A *navarin* is a French ragoût, or stew, made with lamb that is casseroled with young, new-season vegetables. It is also sometimes known as *navarin printanier*, or spring stew.

1. Cut the shoulder of lamb into large pieces and the neck of lamb into slices.
2. Plunge the tomatoes into a bowl of boiling water for 1 minute. Drain and immediately refresh them in a bowl of cold water. Drain again, then peel off the skins, remove the seeds and crush or chop the flesh.
3. Heat the oil in a large flameproof casserole and brown the meat in batches over a high heat, draining the pieces as they brown on a plate lined with kitchen paper.
4. Return the meat to the casserole, lower the heat and sprinkle in the flour. Cook, stirring, for 3 minutes. Season with salt, pepper and a little freshly grated nutmeg. Add the tomatoes, garlic, bouquet garni and enough water to just cover the meat so that it stays moist. Bring to the boil, cover the casserole and simmer for 35 minutes.
5. Meanwhile, scrape the carrots and turnips, then cut the carrots into rounds and the turnips into quarters. Melt the butter in a sauté pan and cook the carrots, turnips and onions until they are just golden.
6. Steam the green beans for 7–8 minutes until almost tender.
7. Add the carrots, turnips, onions and peas to the casserole and stir well to mix. Re-cover the casserole and cook for another 20–25 minutes, adding the green beans 5 minutes before the end of the cooking time, stirring them in gently. Serve immediately straight from the casserole.

STAUB
STAUB

Sugar Tart

TARTE AU SUCRE

Serves 6

Preparation time: 20 mins

Resting time: 2 hours

Cooking time: 35 mins

Ingredients

For the dough

15g (½oz) fresh yeast (or 7g/¼oz sachet fast-action dried yeast)

100ml (3½fl oz) warm milk

250g (9oz) plain flour, plus extra for dusting

pinch of salt

100g (3½oz) butter, melted

2 eggs, beaten

For the topping

100g (3½oz) light soft brown or light muscovado sugar

40g (1½oz) butter, cut into small pieces

150ml (5fl oz) crème fraîche

Sugar beet is grown in abundance in the Pas-de-Calais region and this tart is, without doubt, the most popular of the many made in northern France.

1 First make the dough. If using fresh yeast, dissolve it in the warm milk. Sift the flour into a mixing bowl (then stir in the dried yeast, if using). Make a well in the centre and add the salt, melted butter, eggs and dissolved yeast and milk. Mix to make a dough, then knead until it is smooth and elastic. Shape the dough into a ball, cover with a clean tea towel and leave to rest at room temperature for 1 hour.

2 Line a baking sheet with nonstick baking paper. Roll out the dough on a lightly floured work surface to a 25cm (10-inch) circle and carefully lift it on to the lined baking sheet. Press small hollows all over the dough with your fingertips. Cover and leave to rest for another hour.

3 Preheat the oven to 180°C (350°F), Gas Mark 4. To make the topping, sprinkle the sugar over the top of the dough and dot with the butter. Bake for 30 minutes. Remove the tart from the oven and spread the crème fraîche evenly over the top, then bake for a final 4–6 minutes. Serve the tart warm.

Tip

You can replace the light brown sugar with dark soft brown or dark muscovado sugar, both of which have a stronger taste, and flavour the cream by adding a little vanilla extract or ground cinnamon to it.

Ducasse Waffles

GAUFRES DE DUCASSE

Makes 8–10 waffles

Preparation time: 15 mins

Resting time: 2 hours

Cooking time: 3 mins per batch

Ingredients

12g (½oz) fresh yeast (or half a 7g/¼oz sachet fast-action dried yeast)

125ml (4fl oz) warm milk

250g (9oz) plain flour

pinch of salt

1 egg

125ml (4fl oz) light beer

50g (1¾oz) butter, melted

icing sugar, for dusting

It was during the 15th century that a Flemish artisan invented an iron 'chest' for baking biscuits on both sides over an open fire. Since then, those 'chest biscuits', succeeded by 'wafers' and other types of 'waffles', have delighted generations of foodies of all ages with a sweet tooth.

1. If using fresh yeast, dissolve it in the warm milk. Put the flour in a mixing bowl (then stir in the dried yeast, if using), add the salt, egg and dissolved fresh yeast (if using) and milk and mix together. Then add 125ml (4fl oz) water, the beer and melted butter and mix well – the batter will be quite runny.

2. Cover the bowl with a clean tea towel and leave the batter to rest at room temperature for 2 hours until it has increased in volume.

3. Preheat a waffle maker fitted with 4 large grid plates. Pour a ladleful of batter into the centre, close the waffle maker straight away and flip it over. Leave to cook for 3 minutes. Remove the waffle and cook the remaining batter in the same way. When all the waffles have been cooked, dust them generously with icing sugar and serve immediately.

Fromage Blanc Doughnuts

BEIGNETS CHAMPENOIS AU FROMAGE BLANC

Serves 4

Preparation time: 15 mins

Resting time: 1 hour

Cooking time: 5 mins per batch

Ingredients

250g (9oz) fromage blanc, well drained

1 egg and 1 egg yolk, beaten

50g (1¾oz) caster sugar, plus extra for coating

pinch of salt

70g (2½oz) plain flour

sunflower or groundnut oil, for deep-frying

Fromage blanc is a soft fresh cheese with a slightly tangy flavour that can be difficult to find outside of France. Greek yogurt, ricotta, quark or soured cream all make good substitutes.

1 Work the fromage blanc with a spatula in a mixing bowl, gradually incorporating the beaten egg and egg yolk, the sugar, salt and flour until you have a soft, smooth but not runny dough. Leave the dough to rest for at least 1 hour in the refrigerator.

2 Half-fill a shallow dish with sugar for coating. Heat enough oil for deep-frying in a large pan to 170–180°C (340–350°F). Using a spoon, shape balls of the dough and plunge them, a few at a time, into the hot oil, turning them over several times.

3 Deep-fry the doughnuts for about 5 minutes until they are puffed and golden brown. Remove with a slotted spoon or skimmer and drain on a plate lined with kitchen paper. Roll them in the sugar in the dish until coated and transfer to a serving platter. Serve hot.

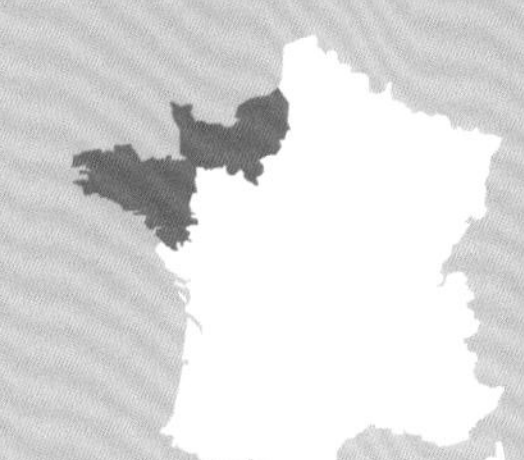

The North West:

Brittany and Normandy

Nantes-style Scallops

COQUILLES SAINT-JACQUES À LA NANTAISE

Serves 4

Preparation time: 30 mins

Cooking time: 10 mins

Ingredients

8 scallops
100g (3½oz) white sandwich bread
150ml (5fl oz) milk
60g (2¼oz) butter
2 shallots, finely sliced
1 garlic clove, very finely chopped
2 tablespoons chopped parsley
dried breadcrumbs, for topping
salt and freshly ground black pepper

Buy scallops in their shells for optimum freshness and so that you can use some of the attractive curved half-shells as serving dishes. Check that all the scallops have tightly closed shells.

1 Open the scallop shells by holding a scallop firmly in your hand with the flat side of the shell next to your thumb, the curved side next to your fingers and the shell resting on the work surface. Slide a knife blade between the 2 halves of the shell at the top and twist until the hinge breaks. Open the shells and discard only the black part attached to the muscle. Remove the round, white scallop meat and orange coral, rinse well and set aside. Wash the 'beards' – the frilly membrane – to remove all the sand, squeeze them well to extract the water and chop very finely. Wash 4 of the curved half-shells thoroughly in hot soapy water, dry and set aside.

2 Preheat the oven to 220°C (425°F), Gas Mark 7. Soak the bread in the milk in a bowl for 5 minutes. Drain and then squeeze it between your fingers. Melt 40g (1½oz) of the butter in a fryng pan and fry the shallots with the garlic over a low heat until they are transparent. Mix with the soaked bread. Add the scallop beards and parsley, season with salt and pepper and stir to mix.

3 Divide half the mixture between the 4 half-shells. Cut each scallop in half horizontally and place in the shells with the corals. Cover with the remaining shallot mixture and sprinkle dried breadcrumbs on top. Cut the remaining butter into small pieces and dot over the breadcrumbs.

4 Bake the scallops for 10 minutes and serve immediately.

SHELLFISH
AND CRUSTACEANS...

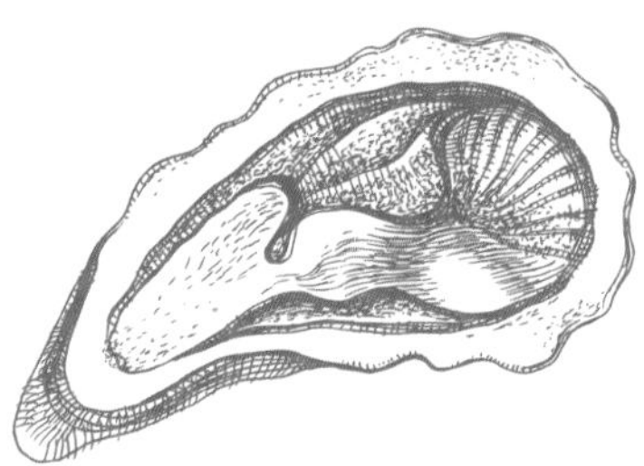

You Either Love 'Em or Hate 'Em!

Whether you are repelled or spellbound by how an oyster looks and its strong flavour of iodine, it is crystal clear that the oyster is divisive! Enjoyed over Christmas in France or with a glass of white wine during the summer months, it is one of the most highly prized shellfish in the country's gastronomic heritage, with no fewer than seven oyster farming basins, mostly on the Atlantic coast. But how do you choose your oyster? There are several ways of differentiating between the various types of oysters: cupped or flat-shelled, *spéciale* (fleshy) or *bien fine* (less fleshy) and numbered to indicate their weight. Cupped oysters, which are the most common, are classified from 0 to 5 – the smaller the number, the heavier the oyster, so a N° 1 oyster will be much bigger than a N° 4 and much more pronounced in the mouth. As for *fine de claire* oysters, this classification refers to a special method of production in the Marennes-Oléron basin where oysters are cultivated in the open sea before being transferred to artificial pools of seawater to be matured for between two and six months prior to harvesting.

The Gourmet's Shellfish

Scallops live on the bottom of the sandy, grassy seabeds of the English Channel and Atlantic Ocean. Harvesting them is highly regulated and is done by mechanically dredging the ocean floor or by what is known as 'hand-diving', carried out by scuba divers. The large shell contains one-part white flesh, which is firm, plump, succulent and called the 'nut', with a separate orange, crescent-shaped coral alongside. It is a genuine zero-waste product, since even the shell can be recycled. For example, the pilgrims of Saint James of Compostela used it as a feeding bowl, which they carried around their necks when not in use. Practical and handy, it is the must-have fashion accessory to take on your next hike (or perhaps not!).

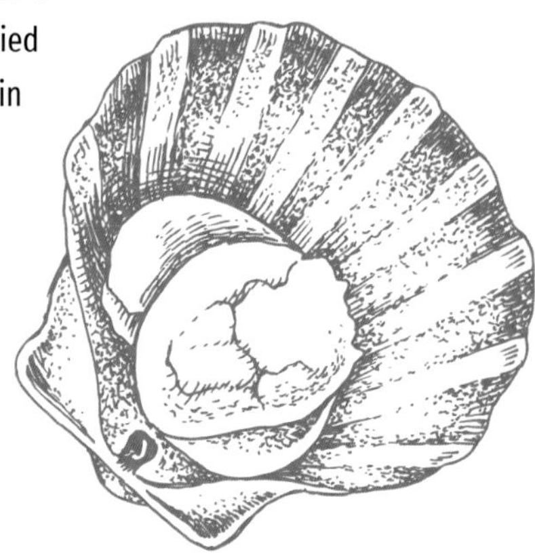

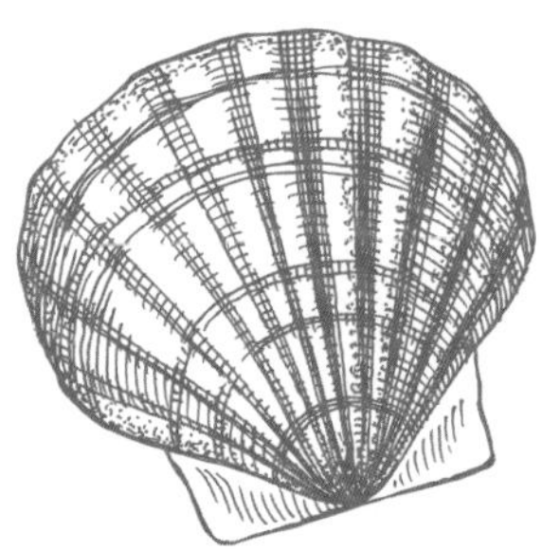

Like a Mussel to its Rock

Small Bouchot mussels have bluish-black shells and are grown on wooden stakes, known as *bouchets*, which are driven into the coastal waters of the Atlantic, and to which the mussels cling naturally, as they would to a rock. This ancient method of cultivation is recognized today as being particularly ecologically friendly and sustainable, with a carbon footprint that is close to zero. These mussels are highly prized for their delicate iodine flavour and firm, fleshy texture. They are frequently eaten in dishes such as a *mouclade*, a speciality of the Charente-Maritime region where they are cooked in a cream and curry sauce (see recipe page 84). Bouchot mussels are also an important source of nutrients such as protein, vitamins and minerals, and relatively low in fat and calories, making them a healthy food choice for seafood lovers. Delicious, nutritionally beneficial and eco-friendly, you can't beat a Bouchot mussel!

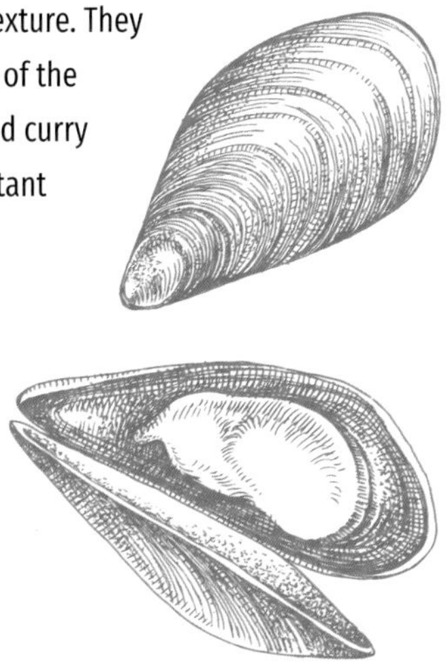

A Spiky Customer!

Sea urchins, small black balls covered in rather intimidating spikes, have a fine, creamy, orange flesh with a highly iodized flavour much appreciated by the discerning seafood lover. However, if you want to fish for a sea urchin yourself, you will have to earn it. It might be easy enough to pick one up from between the rocks on the seabed or along the Mediterranean coast equipped with just a simple mask and snorkel, but beware one of its thorns sinking itself into your flesh! Also, gathering sea urchins is strictly regulated to protect local colonies and ensure sustainable reproduction, meaning you can only collect them between the months of November and April and those dates may differ from one region to another. But what a pleasure it is to open sea urchins on the beach and savour them drizzled with lemon juice, scooping out their flesh with a teaspoon.

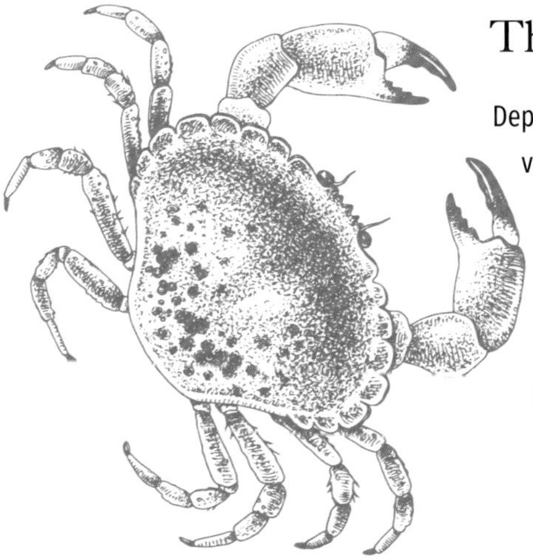

The Who's Who of Touloulou

Depending on its species, age, size and where it is found, this crab is known by various names in the Antilles, including white crab, *boko*, *crabe soleil* (sun crab), red back, *krab a bab* and *touloulou*. Unlike the crabs found along the coastline of the Hexagon (a popular nickname for France. referring to the country's shape), this land crab only reaches the sea during the breeding season, spending the rest of its life living, rabbit-like, in burrows. It is traditionally eaten in the Antilles on Easter Monday.

Chandivert-style Oyster Gratin

GRATIN D'HUÎTRES À LA CHANDIVERT

Serves 4 | **Preparation time: 20 mins** | **Cooking time: 10 mins**

Ingredients

24 oysters (flat-shelled or cupped)

100ml (3½fl oz) dry cider

100ml (3½fl oz) crème fraîche

30g (1oz) dried breadcrumbs

20g (¾oz) butter, cut into small pieces

freshly ground black pepper

thyme sprigs, to garnish (optional)

This gratin was the house speciality of the Chandivert brasserie in Caen, Normandy, which was famous before the Second World War. The brasserie no longer exists, but it is memorialized in this dish.

1 To open the oysters, wrap a tea towel around one hand so that you can grip the oyster firmly and to protect your hand in case the knife slips. Using an oyster knife (or another knife with a short, sturdy blade), position the point of it at the base of the hinge and, exerting pressure, twist the knife. Lever it upwards, this time without pressure on it, or twist the knife blade to prise the hinge apart. Remove the oysters from their shells, reserving the liquid inside. Place the oysters back in their half-shells. Season with a grind of black pepper.

2 Strain the reserved liquid from the oysters into a small saucepan and boil over a high heat to reduce it by half. Whisk in the cider and crème fraîche, lower the heat and simmer gently until you have a creamy sauce.

3 Preheat the oven to 180°C (350°F), Gas Mark 4. Coat the oysters in their shells with the sauce and sprinkle with the breadcrumbs, then dot the butter over the breadcrumbs. Bake for 10 minutes and then serve immediately, garnished with thyme sprigs if you wish.

Tip

You can also make individual gratins in ovenproof ramekins.

Buckwheat Galettes

GALETTES DE BLÉ NOIR

Makes 8–10 galettes

Preparation time: 10 mins

Resting time: 1 hour

Cooking time: 4 mins per galette

Ingredients

300g (10½oz) buckwheat flour

pinch of salt

1 large egg, beaten

about 750ml (1⅓ pints) cold water

oil, for greasing

fillings of your choice, such as grated cheese, chopped ham and sautéed sliced mushrooms, wilted baby spinach leaves or sliced tomatoes

In the 15th century, Duchess Anne decided to cultivate buckwheat in her Duchy of Brittany. This fast-growing pseudocereal, also known as *sarrasin* (in memory of the Crusades), would, in different forms, provide Bretons with a staple part of their daily diet until the mid-19th century when white wheat flour gradually replaced it. The 2–3mm (1⁄16–1⁄18-inch) thick galette (any thinner, it would be a buckwheat crepe) is a speciality of eastern Brittany and is delicious served with a wide range of savoury fillings.

1 Sift the flour into a mixing bowl. Make a well in the centre, add the salt and egg and pour in a little of the water. Stir to mix with a balloon whisk, gradually mixing in the rest of the water until you have a smooth batter.

2 Cover the bowl with a clean tea towel and leave the batter to rest in a cool place for 1 hour.

3 To cook the galettes, oil a large frying pan and place over a medium-high heat. Pour in a ladleful of the batter and spread it in a thin layer with a wooden spatula. Leave to cook for about 3 minutes, then carefully release it from the pan with a metal spatula without turning it over (traditionally galettes are only cooked on one side so that they remain soft).

4 Add your chosen filling ingredients to the centre of each galette as it cooks, still without turning it over, and let the filling heat through. Fold the edges of the galette inwards over the filling before serving.

Vallée d'Auge Chicken

POULET VALLÉE D'AUGE

Serves 6

Preparation time: 30 mins

Cooking time: 45 mins

Ingredients

1 corn-fed chicken, weighing about 1.8kg (4lb)

100g (3½oz) butter

3 tablespoons Calvados

50g (1¾oz) shallots, quartered

150ml (5fl oz) dry cider

a few sage leaves, plus an extra sprig to garnish

250g (9oz) button mushrooms, trimmed and sliced

200ml (7fl oz) crème fraîche

salt and freshly ground black pepper

To make this dish, cooks in Normandy would use a plump, mature Crèvecoeur, a chicken from the Calvados area, or a Houdan chicken, both of which are historic local breeds with a full, rich flavour.

1 Cut the chicken into joints.

2 Melt half the butter in a flameproof casserole over a medium heat and fry the chicken joints until golden brown on both sides. Drain the fat from the casserole, add the Calvados and flambé (set alight briefly). Season with salt and pepper, stir in the shallots and deglaze the pan with the cider. Add the sage leaves, then cover and simmer for about 40 minutes until the chicken is cooked through.

3 Meanwhile, heat the rest of the butter in a pan over a medium heat, add the mushrooms and cover the pan with a lid, then cook for 3–4 minutes, stirring from time to time. Remove the lid and leave to cook until the liquid evaporates.

4 About 5 minutes before the end of the chicken cooking time, add the crème fraîche, stirring it into the cooking juices until smooth. Add the mushrooms and simmer over a gentle heat.

5 Remove the chicken joints from the casserole and transfer them to a hot serving dish. Taste the sauce, adding more seasoning if necessary, then spoon it over the chicken. Serve accompanied with hash browns or fried potatoes, garnished with a sage sprig.

Mortagne Black Pudding with Apples

BOUDIN DE MORTAGNE AUX POMMES

Serves 4

Preparation time: 10 mins

Cooking time: 15 mins

Ingredients

4–6 apples

100g (3½oz) butter

4 pieces of black pudding, weighing about 200g (7oz) each

salt and freshly ground black pepper

The gastronomic speciality of Mortagne-au-Perche (in the Orne department of Normandy) is black pudding – or blood sausage – and for more than 50 years, the city has held an international competition where black puddings from all over France, the rest of Europe and other parts of the world compete for the prestigious title of best blood sausage.

1 Peel the apples, remove the cores and seeds and cut into thick slices.

2 Melt half the butter in a frying pan, add the apples and cook them over a very gentle heat for about 15 minutes until they are golden brown. Season with salt and pepper.

3 Meanwhile, melt the rest of the butter in another frying pan and fry the pieces of black pudding over a higher heat for about 10 minutes, turning them over several times.

4 Transfer the black pudding to individual hot serving dishes or one large platter and spoon the apples alongside. Serve immediately.

Cider-braised Gammon

JAMBON BRAISÉ AU CIDRE

Serves 6

Preparation time: 15 mins

Soaking time: 24 hours

Cooking time: 1 hour

Ingredients

1.2kg (2lb 10oz) unsmoked or smoked boneless gammon joint

1.5 litres (2¾ pints) dry cider

1 bouquet garni

150g (5½oz) butter

3 tablespoons apple cider vinegar

salt and freshly ground black pepper

The type of ham used in France for this dish is *demi-sel*, literally 'half-salted' or lightly salt-cured, gammon being the nearest widely available equivalent in the UK, or fresh ham in the USA. Instead of gammon, you could use a joint of cooked ham on the bone. In that case, omit steps 1–3 and replace the gammon cooking liquid in step 5 with cider.

1. The day before, soak the gammon joint in a large bowl of cold water for 24 hours to remove the excess salt, changing the water several times. Drain the joint.

2. The next day, put the gammon in a large saucepan with the cider and bouquet garni. Heat gently until the cider is almost boiling, then poach, with the liquid just rippling, for 45 minutes. Remove the pan from the heat and let the gammon cool in the cooking juices.

3. Drain the gammon, reserving the cooking juices (discard the bouquet garni), and cut off the rind and fat.

4. Cut the gammon into slices about 1cm (½ inch) thick. Heat 30g (1oz) of the butter in a frying pan and brown the gammon slices in batches on both sides over a medium heat. As they brown, remove them from the pan, arrange on a serving plate and keep warm. Discard the cooking fat in the frying pan.

5. Return the pan to a high heat and deglaze with the vinegar, scraping the bottom of the pan well to incorporate any juices sticking to it. Cook for a few minutes, then pour in a glass of the reserved cooking juices, bring to the boil and reduce by about one-third. Cut the remaining butter into small pieces and whisk in gradually. Taste and adjust the seasoning.

6. Spoon a little of the sauce over the gammon slices and serve the rest alongside. Accompany with leeks steamed with butter and boiled or steamed new potatoes.

Breton Stew with Buckwheat Dumplings

KIG HA FARZ

Serves 8

Preparation time: 30 mins

Cooking time: 4 hours

Ingredients

1 small cabbage

300g (10½oz) carrots

3 onions

1 celery stick

1.5kg (3lb 5oz) braising beef (shin or chuck steak), cut into pieces

1 bouquet garni

750g (1lb 10oz) pork belly, cut into pieces

salt and freshly ground black pepper

chopped parsley, to garnish

For the farz (dumplings)

200g (7oz) buckwheat flour

2 eggs

200ml (7fl oz) milk

200ml (7fl oz) crème fraîche

This traditional dish comes from Finistère in Brittany, *kig ha farz* literally translating as 'meat and flour' from the Breton dialect, with *farz* being the buckwheat dumplings. Different meats can be used, in this recipe a combination of pork and beef.

1 Remove any damaged or discoloured outer leaves from the cabbage. Trim the carrots and onions, then cut all the vegetables into large pieces. Put them in a flameproof casserole with the beef and bouquet garni. Cover with plenty of water and bring to the boil, skimming regularly to remove the foam. Season with salt and pepper and cook over a very low heat so that the water is just rippling for 2 hours.

2 Prepare the *farz*. Sift the flour into a mixing bowl. Beat the eggs with 1 teaspoon of salt, then add to the flour, mixing well with a spatula. Heat the milk and crème fraîche in a pan, then gradually pour into the bowl, stirring continuously until you have a smooth, fairly soft dough.

3 Shape the dough into 8 or more balls and wrap them in squares of muslin, tying them closed with kitchen string.

4 Add the bags of dough to the casserole, submerging them in the cooking liquid, and continue to simmer gently for 1 hour. Add the pork belly and cook for another hour. Sprinkle over some chopped parsley to garnish.

5 Transfer the meats and vegetables to a hot serving dish, unwrap the *farz* and arrange around the dish. Serve the cooking liquid in soup tureens.

Tip

This Breton-style *pot-au-feu* with dumplings is a unique dish. You can serve the *farz* first with the cooking liquid and bring the meats and vegetables to the table afterwards or serve everything at the same time, adding some of the cooking liquid to individual serving plates so that the meat and vegetables are not dry.

Mussels in White Wine

MOULES À LA MARINIÈRE

Serves 4–6

Preparation time: 20 mins

Cooking time: 8 mins

Ingredients

3kg (6lb 8oz) mussels

30g (1oz) butter

1 large onion, chopped

1 shallot, chopped

200–300ml (7–10fl oz) dry white wine

1 thyme sprig

½ bay leaf

salt and freshly ground black pepper

chopped parsley, to garnish

Since Normandy is the largest mussel-farming area in France and Brittany is in second place, it's hardly surprising that this easy-to-cook dish is hugely popular both with locals and tourists. The traditional accompaniment is a bowl of crisp chips or wholemeal bread.

1. To prepare the mussels, pull away the thread-like 'beards' attached to the shells and scrape the shells under cold water with a small knife to remove any barnacles. Avoid soaking the mussels in cold water, as this will make them open. If any have opened, tap the shells gently and they should close again. If not, discard them, along with any mussels that have cracked or broken shells.
2. Melt the butter in a lidded, deep-sided, wide pan, add the onion and shallot and fry over a very gentle heat for 1–2 minutes.
3. Tip in the mussels, followed by the wine. Season with salt and pepper and add the thyme sprig and bay leaf half. Cover and cook them over a high heat for 6 minutes, stirring frequently and shaking the pan from time to time.
4. When all the mussel shells have opened, transfer them from the pan with a slotted spoon or skimmer into hot serving bowls. Remove and discard the thyme and bay leaf half, as well as any mussels that have remained tightly closed. Pour the cooking liquid over the mussels and stir to mix. Sprinkle with chopped parsley to garnish and serve immediately.

Tip

You can strain the cooking liquid and whisk 3 tablespoons of crème fraîche into it before pouring it over the mussels.

Breton Fish Stew

COTRIADE

Serves 6

Preparation time: 30 mins

Cooking time: 40 mins

Ingredients

1.5kg (3lb 5oz) different types of fish, including conger eel and a mix of oily and white varieties such as mackerel, wrasse, whiting and pollock, scaled where necessary, cleaned and gutted

50g (1¾oz) lightly salted butter

2 onions, chopped

6 medium potatoes, peeled and cut into thick slices if large

salt and freshly ground black pepper

For the dressing

1 tablespoon hot mustard

3 tablespoons cider vinegar

135ml (4½fl oz) olive oil

2 tablespoons chopped parsley

This Breton speciality is made from different types of fish, usually a mix of oily and white varieties, plus potatoes. As with the bouillabaisse of Marseille, it was traditionally cooked by fishermen to fortify them when they had returned to port and unloaded their catch.

1. Rinse the fish and pat dry with kitchen paper. Cut them into pieces or slices and leave the smallest ones whole.
2. Melt the butter in a flameproof casserole and fry the onions over a medium heat until translucent. Add the potatoes, pour in enough water to cover them and season with salt and pepper. Bring to the boil, then lower the heat and simmer for 10 minutes.
3. Meanwhile, prepare the dressing. Mix together the mustard and vinegar in a bowl and season with salt. Gradually drizzle in the oil in a thin stream, whisking continuously with a fork so that the sauce emulsifies. Add the parsley and pour the mixture into a serving dish.
4. Add the conger eel to the casserole and continue cooking for 10 minutes. Add the other firm-fleshed fish (such as mackerel and pollock) and cook for another 5–6 minutes. Finally, add the more delicate fish (such as whiting) and leave to cook over a low heat for 4 more minutes.
5. Carefully lift the fish out of the casserole with a skimmer and transfer to a hot serving platter. Arrange the potatoes around the fish and add 2 ladles of the cooking liquid to keep the fish moist. Pour over a few spoonfuls of the dressing. Serve the soup separately, accompanied with slices of toast.

Oven-baked Sardines

SARDINES AU PLAT

Serves 4

Preparation time: 20 mins

Cooking time: 10–12 mins

Ingredients

24 fresh sardines
40g (1½oz) butter
4 shallots, sliced lengthways into wedges
juice of 1 lemon
½ glass dry white wine
a few parsley sprigs, roughly chopped
salt and freshly ground black pepper

These small oily fish are rich in nutrients and they are an excellent source of omega-3 fatty acids, vitamins and minerals. As well as being baked in the oven, the sardines can also be fried, grilled or barbecued.

1. Clean and gut the sardines, leaving the heads and tails on or removing them as you prefer. Season the sardines with salt and pepper.
2. Preheat the oven to its highest setting. Grease a large roasting tin with 10g (¼oz) of the butter and spread half the shallots over it. Season with salt.
3. Lay the sardines in the dish, top with the remaining shallots and drizzle over the lemon juice. Pour over the wine. Cut the rest of the butter into small pieces and dot over the sardines. Bake for 10–12 minutes.
4. Scatter the chopped parsley over the sardines as soon as they come out of the oven and serve immediately.

Sea Bass Baked with a Salt Crust

BAR EN CROÛTE DE SEL DE GUÉRANDE

Serves 4

Preparation time: 15 mins

Cooking time: 35–45 mins

Ingredients

1 sea bass, weighing about 1.2–1.5kg (2lb 10oz–3lb 5oz)

2kg (4lb 8oz) coarse sel de Guérande

For the Hollandaise sauce

3 tablespoons white wine vinegar

4 egg yolks

250g (9oz) butter, melted

salt and freshly ground white pepper

Baking sea bass in a salt crust seals in all its juices as the fish cooks, ensuring the flesh remains beautifully moist. Sel de Guérande is a coarse sea salt that is gathered by hand from the marshes around the village of Guérande in Brittany and then dried in the sun during the months of July and August.

1 Clean and gut the sea bass without removing the scales. Rinse and carefully pat it dry with kitchen paper.

2 Preheat the oven to 240°C (475°F), Gas Mark 9. Spread out half the salt in an even layer in an ovenproof dish or roasting tin lined with a sheet of foil. Lay the fish on top and cover it completely with the rest of the salt. Bake for 35–45 minutes.

3 While the fish is cooking, prepare the Hollandaise sauce. Pour the vinegar into a small, heavy-based saucepan and reduce it by half over a high heat. Remove the pan from the heat and leave the vinegar to cool until it is lukewarm. Create a bain-marie by half-filling a roasting tin with moderately hot water (the temperature of the water must be no higher than 80°C/176°F). Stand the saucepan in the roasting tin and add 3 tablespoons of cold water and the egg yolks to the vinegar and whisk until the mixture thickens a little. Gradually pour in the melted butter, still whisking continuously. Season the sauce with salt and pepper and set aside.

4 When the fish is cooked, remove it from the oven, and leave to rest for 10 minutes. Carefully lift away the salt crust and discard it. Peel the skin off the fish, brushing away any remaining salt. Lift the flesh off the bones in large pieces to serve. Accompany with boiled or steamed new potatoes and the Hollandaise sauce.

Sweet Breton Cake

KOUIGN-AMANN

Serves 6	Preparation time: 40 mins	Resting time: 1¼ hours	Cooking time: 30 mins

200ml (7fl oz) warm water

200g (7oz) lightly salted butter, softened, and 50g (1¾oz) for greasing

10g (¼oz) fresh yeast

10g (¼oz) lightly salted butter, melted

300g (10½oz) plain flour

200g (7oz) sugar, plus 50g (1¾oz) for the tin

Ingredients

10g (¼oz) fresh yeast (or half a 7g/¼oz sachet fast-action dried yeast)

200ml (7fl oz) warm water

300g (10½oz) plain flour, plus extra for dusting

10g (¼oz) lightly salted butter, melted, plus 200g (7oz), softened, and 50g (1¾oz) for greasing

200g (7oz) sugar, plus 50g (1¾oz) for the tin

This cake gets its name from the Breton dialect words for 'cake' (*kouign*) and 'butter' (*amann*). The yeast dough is layered with butter and sugar and then slowly baked in the oven so that the sugar caramelizes and the steam produced by the water in the butter makes the cake rise in layers.

1 If using fresh yeast, dissolve it in the warm water.

2 Sift the flour into a mixing bowl (then stir in the dried yeast, if using). Make a well in the centre and add the dissolved fresh yeast (if using) and water and the melted butter. Mix to make a dough, then knead for about 10 minutes until soft and smooth.

3 Cover the bowl with a clean tea towel and leave the dough to rise in a warm place for about 1 hour until it has doubled in volume.

4 Thinly roll out the dough on a lightly floured work surface into a circle so that it resembles a large pancake. Spread the softened butter over it, leaving a 2cm (¾-inch) margin around the edge. Sprinkle the 200g (7oz) of sugar over the butter.

5 Fold the dough in half then in half again to form a triangle.

6 Preheat the oven to 200°C (400°F), Gas Mark 6. Generously grease a 22–24cm (8½–9½-inch) round shallow cake tin with the remaining butter and coat it with the remaining sugar.

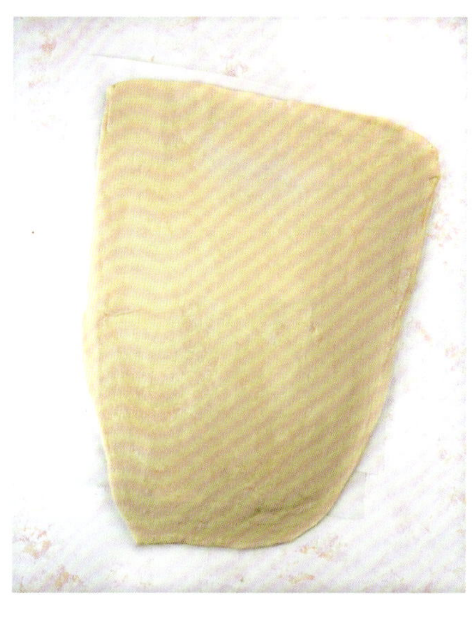

7 Leave the dough to rest for a few minutes and then roll it out again.

8 Fold the rolled-out dough into 4, roll it out again into a long rectangle and cut the rectangle horizontally into 8 equal strips.

9 Roll up each strip from one short end into a snail-like spiral. Place the rolls side by side in the cake tin and bake for 30 minutes, covering the top of the cake with a sheet of foil towards the end of the baking time if it starts to brown too much. Turn out the cake while it is still hot and serve warm.

Breton Far with Prunes

FAR AUX PRUNEAUX

Serves 6

Preparation time: 10 mins

Soaking time: 1 hour

Cooking time: 45 mins

Ingredients

200g (7oz) prunes
500ml (18fl oz) boiling hot black tea
100ml (3½fl oz) Armagnac or dark rum
100g (3½oz) plain flour, plus extra for dusting
120g (4¼oz) sugar
4 eggs
500ml (18fl oz) milk
butter, for greasing

This French dessert cake consists of a rich custard studded with brandy-soaked prunes that is baked in the oven until set. Originally from Brittany, *far* is now popular all over France and legend has it that the recipe originated when the fishermen from Brittany traded their catch for Agen prunes – and, no doubt, brandy from Armagnac as well.

1 Stone the prunes, if necessary. Soak them in the hot tea and half the Armagnac (or rum) in a bowl for about 1 hour until they are plump and swollen, then drain.

2 Sift the flour into a mixing bowl and stir in the sugar. Mix in the eggs, one at a time, stirring the mixture with a wooden spoon until you have a smooth batter. Gradually pour in the milk and the rest of the Armagnac (or rum), stirring thoroughly until incorporated.

3 Preheat the oven to 190°C (375°F), Gas Mark 5. Generously grease a shallow ovenproof dish with butter and dust with flour. Pour the batter into the dish and arrange the prunes on top. Bake for 45 minutes, covering the top with a sheet of foil towards the end of the baking time if it is starting to brown too much. Serve straight from the dish.

Tip

This *far* with prunes originates from the Quiberon region of Brittany and is the most popular, but *fars* that have raisins or pears added are also popular.

Crepes

CRÊPES

Serves 6

Preparation time: 10 mins

Resting time: 2 hours

Cooking time: 2–3 mins per crepe

Ingredients

250g (9oz) plain flour

500ml (18fl oz) milk

25g (1oz) butter, plus extra for greasing

3 eggs

pinch of salt

The origin of crepes goes back as far as the 13th century when they were being made in Brittany, likely using buckwheat flour.

1 Sift the flour into a mixing bowl and make a well in the centre. Pour in half the milk and mix by gradually stirring in the flour from around the sides towards the centre.

2 Melt the butter in a small saucepan over a gentle heat. Break the eggs into another bowl and beat them together. Gradually stir the eggs into the flour mixture until incorporated, then add the melted butter and salt. Continue to stir until the batter is completely smooth. Gradually pour in the rest of the milk, stirring continuously to avoid any lumps forming. The batter must be free-flowing but not runny. Cover the bowl with a clean tea towel and leave to rest for 2 hours.

3 Lightly grease a nonstick frying pan with butter and place over a medium-high heat. Pour a small ladleful of batter into it. Tilt the pan in all directions so that the batter spreads out in a thin even layer. Return the pan to the heat, and when the batter is no longer shiny on top, release the edges from the pan with a spatula and flip the crepe over. Cook the other side for 1 minute or until the crepe is golden in colour. Slide the crepe from the pan on to a large plate. Lightly grease the pan again and cook more crepes in the same way until you have used up all the batter. Serve hot with sugar and lemon juice or, for an indulgent treat, a spoonful of salted caramel (see recipe page 78).

Tip

The secret to making perfect crepes lies in letting the batter rest and getting its consistency right. Dip a ladle in the batter, turn it over and run your finger through the batter coating the rounded side of the ladle. If the line made by your finger remains clean and does not close up straight away, the batter is the desired consistency and not too runny. If it is too thick, dilute it with a little water or milk just before cooking the crepes.

FRENCH BONBONS

...ENJOY!

The Star of Montélimar

There is one thing about Nougat de Montélimar you can rely on – it will stick to your teeth for a long time. But what a sweet treat this nougat is! Made with honey and almonds, it is one of the most recognizable specialities of Provence and even has the honour of being included in the list of the 13 traditional desserts served on Christmas Eve. Several other Mediterranean countries make their own versions, such as *turron* in Spain, *torrone* in Italy and *mandolato* in Greece.

The Aix-Ellent Calisson

Should you find yourself passing through the Bouches-du-Rhône region of southern France, give in to temptation in the form of the Calisson d'Aix. This small, lozenge-shaped delicacy, made from almonds and candied melon and orange, is *the* speciality of the small, pretty town of Aix-en-Provence. It was invented in the 15th century by the pastry chef of the king, René d'Anjou, a great monastic figure, on the occasion of his marriage to Jeanne de Laval. Every year on the first Sunday in September, the town celebrates the blessing of the Calisson with a festival that includes a procession in traditional dress, Provençal dances and the distribution of these small treats to Aix residents with a sweet tooth.

Small Error, Huge Success!

Bétises de Cambrai are a boiled sweet made in the town of Cambrai in the Hauts-de-France region. *Bétise* means 'nonsense' or a 'stupid mistake'. This white, pillow-shaped sweet, streaked with coloured sugar, came about due to a confectioner accidentally pouring mint into his sweet mixture, hence its name. He sold the sweets to his customers without saying a word so as not to waste what he had made and they were as delighted with this new and original indulgence as with the traditional version. Today the Bétise has diversified and is now made in a variety of different flavours that range from apple and lemon to raspberry and violet.

Pink City, Violet Sweet

It would be hard to create anything more poetic than the Violettes de Toulouse or candied Toulouse violets – little sweets made from the petals of the fresh flowers. Violets, which grow in the area around the southern city of Toulouse, are picked in full bloom around March and their petals are then crystallized in sugar. This can only be done by hand, as it is a very delicate process due to the fragility of the flowers. It is important not to confuse them with Toulouse *violette* bonbons, which are made like traditional sweets.

Grandmothers' Favourite

The Vichy pastille was created in 1825 in the spa town of Vichy, located in the north of the Auvergne-Rhône-Alpes region. Made from sugar and mineral salts from Vichy's thermal springs, the pastille is said to improve digestion and freshen the breath, thanks to its mild minty flavour. A real institution in the city, it is however considered by some as a rather unfashionable sweet, but it is still a treat worth the detour!

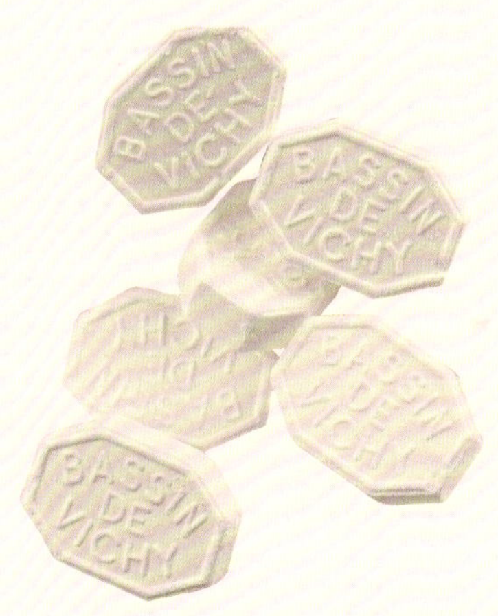

Funny Little Berlingots

The Carpentras *berlingot* ('humbug' in English) is shaped like a small, coloured pyramid streaked with lines of white sugar and made from candied sugar syrup. As with the pastilles from Vichy, berlingots were originally sold by the apothecaries in the Avignon region for their medicinal benefits, but you can be confident that today you will have no need of a prescription to get your hands on these addictive little sweets!

Salted Caramel

CARAMEL AU BEURRE-SALÉ

Makes about 280g (10oz) | **Preparation time: 5 mins** | **Cooking time: 15–20 mins**

Ingredients

150g (5½oz) sugar

juice of ½ lemon, strained

100ml (3½fl oz) single cream

25g (1oz) lightly salted (or salted) butter, well chilled and cut into small pieces

Salted caramel is quick and simple to put together, and you will likely have all the ingredients to hand. Try it on crepes (see recipe page 74).

1 Melt the sugar with the lemon juice in a heavy-based saucepan. Do this over a low heat to avoid crystals forming. Do not add any water and, most importantly, do not stir. Using a pastry brush dipped in water, regularly brush down the sides of the saucepan to remove any splashes.

2 Meanwhile, gently heat the cream, without boiling, in a separate small heavy-based saucepan.

3 Once the sugar has completely melted, boil the syrup until it is golden in colour. Remove it from the heat to stop further cooking and drizzle the hot cream into it in a steady stream, stirring continuously. Once the cream is evenly mixed in, add the pieces of butter and mix with a wooden spatula until you have a smooth sauce.

Tip

The caramel will stay soft if left at room temperature. It can be spread into a shortcrust pastry case and topped with a layer of chocolate ganache or other tart filling – lemon, orange, pear, apple, pineapple – the choice is yours. It will keep for three days in the refrigerator but be warned that it will harden, which provides the perfect excuse to finish it quickly!

The Atlantic Seaboard

Salt Cod Salad with Potatoes

SALADE DE MORUE AUX POMMES DE TERRE

Serves 6

Preparation time: 30 mins

Soaking time: 24 hours

Cooking time: 30 mins

Ingredients

1kg (2lb 4oz) dried salt cod
500g (1lb 2oz) waxy potatoes, washed
6 eggs
6 tablespoons olive oil
2 tablespoons sherry vinegar
1 small bunch of parsley, chopped
salt and freshly ground black pepper

Dried salt cod might not look very appetizing on the fishmonger's slab, but once it has been rehydrated and cooked it has a firm, flaky texture and mild, delicate flavour.

1 The day before, cut the salt cod into large pieces and soak them in a bowl of cold water for 24 hours to remove the excess salt, changing the water several times.

2 The next day, cook the unpeeled potatoes in a saucepan of salted boiling water until they are tender. Drain and leave them to cool, then peel off their skins and slice into rounds. Hard-boil the eggs, cool under cold running water and shell them.

3 Drain the salt cod pieces, place them in a flameproof casserole and pour over cold water so that the cod is well covered. Heat gently, and as soon as the first tremble appears on the surface of the water, switch off the heat and cover the casserole. Leave the fish in its cooking water for 5 more minutes.

4 Drain the cod, remove the skin and bones and flake the flesh.

5 Prepare a vinaigrette by whisking the oil and vinegar together, seasoning it with pepper but not salt.

6 Slice the potatoes into rounds. Mix the salt cod flakes with the sliced potatoes and divide between 6 bowls. Cut the hard-boiled eggs lengthways into quarters and arrange over the cod and potatoes. Spoon over the vinaigrette and scatter over the chopped parsley.

Mussels in a Creamy Curry Sauce

MOUCLADE

Serves 4 | **Preparation time: 40 mins** | **Cooking time: 20 mins**

Ingredients

2kg (4lb 8oz) mussels (preferably Bouchot – see page 47)

2 glasses dry white wine

50g (1¾oz) shallots, chopped

2 garlic cloves, chopped

1 bouquet garni

2 tablespoons double cream

large pinch of saffron threads

1 level tablespoon curry powder

pinch of cayenne pepper

2 egg yolks

1 tablespoon chopped parsley

A speciality of the Charente-Maritime region of western France and in particular its capital, the coastal city of La Rochelle, *mouclade* is a warming winter dish of plump mussels cooked in a delicately spiced rich cream sauce.

1. To prepare the mussels, pull away the thread-like 'beards' attached to the shells and scrape the shells under cold water with a small knife to remove any barnacles. Avoid soaking the mussels in cold water, as this will make them open. If any have opened, tap the shells gently and they should close again. If not, discard them along with any mussels that have cracked or broken shells.
2. Put the mussels in a large, lidded pan, add the wine, shallots, garlic and bouquet garni. Cover and cook over a high heat until all the shells have opened, shaking the pan from time to time. Discard any that remain tightly closed.
3. Drain the mussels in a colander over a large bowl, reserving the cooking juices. Remove the top shell of each mussel and arrange them, one by one, in a large shallow serving dish. Keep warm while you prepare the sauce.
4. Strain the cooking juices into a saucepan and add the cream and saffron. Reduce over a gentle heat before adding the curry powder and cayenne. Remove from the heat and whisk in the egg yolks.
5. Pour the sauce over the mussels, sprinkle with the chopped parsley and serve immediately.

Challans Chicken with Salt-marsh Samphire

POULET FERMIER DE CHALLANS AUX SALICORNES DES MARAIS

Serves 6 | **Preparation time: 30 mins** | **Cooking time: 1 hour**

Ingredients

1 free-range chicken, preferably corn-fed, weighing about 2kg (4lb 8oz)

2 tablespoons plain flour

50g (1¾oz) butter

3 tablespoons oil

3 tablespoons best-quality red wine vinegar, such as aged Bordeaux (or sherry vinegar)

500ml (18fl oz) chicken stock

300g (10½oz) marsh samphire

250ml (9fl oz) crème fraîche

coarse sea salt and coarsely ground black pepper

The commune of Challans in the Vendée department of the Pays de la Loire is famous for its Label Rouge (or Red Label, indicating a product superior in quality within its category) chickens. Reared on grain in the open air, they have tender, succulent flesh.

1 Cut the chicken into 8 or 10 pieces and dust them lightly with the flour. Heat the butter and oil in a sauté pan and fry the chicken pieces over a low heat until golden brown all over. As they brown, transfer them to a flameproof casserole where they will finish cooking.

2 Discard the fat in the sauté pan and deglaze the pan with the vinegar, scraping the bottom of the pan to dissolve and incorporate the juices. Add the stock, bring to the boil and then pour it into the casserole. Season very lightly with salt (samphire is usually very salty) and the coarsely ground black pepper.

3 Cover the casserole and cook over a very low heat for 35 minutes, stirring from time to time.

4 Meanwhile, cook the samphire in a saucepan of boiling water for about 10 minutes, without adding salt to the cooking water. Taste before draining the samphire: it must still be a little crunchy.

5 Add the crème fraîche and samphire to the casserole. Bring back to the boil and serve in a deep, preferably preheated dish, sprinkled with coarse sea salt and pepper.

Worth knowing

Samphire is a very common plant on coastal marshes. Only its fleshy, intensely green stalks and leaves are edible. After picking, samphire can also be pickled in the same way as cornichons (gherkins) and used as a condiment.

Pigeons with Aromatic Herbs

PIGEONNEAUX AUX HERBILLETTES

Serves 4

Preparation time: 30 mins

Cooking time: 1 hour

Ingredients

4 young squab pigeons, with their livers and giblets

200g (7oz) cured ham

½ bunch of chives, chopped

½ bunch of parsley, chopped

½ bunch of chervil, chopped, plus extra to garnish

leaves from 1 thyme sprig

leaves from 1 rosemary sprig, chopped

2 garlic cloves, chopped

100g (3½oz) butter, softened

1 egg yolk

5–6 shallots, chopped

250g (9oz) button mushrooms, trimmed and diced

150ml (5fl oz) dry white wine

150ml (5fl oz) chicken stock

1 tablespoon oil

salt and freshly ground black pepper

Young farmed squab pigeons are used to make this recipe, as their meat is tender, lean and has a richer flavour than other types of poultry.

1 Set aside the livers and the giblets of the pigeons. Using a chopper or a large, heavy chef's knife, break the backbones of the birds and press down to flatten them well.

2 Remove any rind from the ham. Chop the ham and pigeon livers and giblets and mix together in a bowl. Add all the herbs, the garlic, half the butter and the egg yolk, season with salt and pepper and mix together well.

3 Melt the remaining butter in a sauté pan, add the shallots and fry them for 2–3 minutes. Add the mushrooms, stir to mix and cook them over a high heat for 5 minutes, stirring several times. Season with salt and pepper.

4 Pour in the wine and stock, bring to the boil and boil for about 3 minutes. Lower the heat to medium, add the chopped ham mixture and stir to mix, then cover the pan and cook for about 20 minutes.

5 Meanwhile, heat the oil in a flameproof casserole over a medium heat and fry the pigeons until golden brown all over. Cover and leave to cook for 10 minutes on each side (or for 6–8 minutes if you prefer the meat pink).

6 Drain the pigeons and transfer them to a hot serving plate. Spoon the herb mixture over them, sprinkle with extra chervil to garnish and serve hot with roasted baby potatoes.

Tip

The preparation of the herb sauce needs to be done quite quickly. If the sauce is too liquid, uncover the pan towards the end of the cooking time so that it reduces.

PALLARES
SOLSONA

Chalais Veal Shank with Pineau des Charentes

JARRET DE VEAU DE CHALAIS AU PINEAU DES CHARENTES

Serves 6 | **Preparation time: 40 mins** | **Cooking time: 1½ hours**

Ingredients

1.5kg (3lb 5oz) veal shank cut into round slices 3cm (1¼in) thick by your butcher

plain flour, for dusting

3 large leeks

700g (1lb 9oz) tomatoes

100g (3½oz) butter

3 carrots, sliced into rounds

2 tablespoons oil

200ml (7fl oz) Pineau des Charentes

2 garlic cloves, peeled

1 bouquet garni

salt and freshly ground black pepper

This dish is a speciality of the town of Chalais in the Charente region, which is famous for its veal, and every July a festival is held there celebrating this beautifully tender white meat. Pineau des Charentes is the local aperitif, a fortified wine made from grape juice to which Cognac eau-de-vie is added before being matured.

1 Dust the slices of veal with flour, shaking off the excess. Peel the outer layers from the leeks so that only the tender white and green parts remain, then clean and finely chop them.

2 Plunge the tomatoes into a saucepan of boiling water for 1 minute. Drain and cool them in a bowl of cold water, then drain again and peel off the skins. Remove the seeds and roughly chop the tomatoes.

3 Melt 70g (2½oz) of the butter in a flameproof casserole and cook the leeks and carrots over a low heat without letting them colour. Add the tomatoes and continue to cook until they break down and are soft.

4 Meanwhile, heat the remaining butter and the oil in a frying pan and fry the veal slices on both sides until they are golden brown. Season with salt and pepper, then transfer the slices to the casserole where they will finish cooking.

5 Pour the Pineau des Charentes into the frying pan and stir with a wooden spoon to incorporate the juices sticking to the bottom of the pan. Bring to the boil and pour into the casserole. Add the garlic cloves and bouquet garni and adjust the seasoning, if necessary. Cover and simmer over a low heat for at least 1 hour or until the veal is tender. Remove the bouquet garni and serve straight from the casserole.

Beef Daube Saintongeaise

DAUBE DE 'BEU' SAINTONGEAISE

Serves 6	Preparation time: 30 mins	Cooking time: 3½–4½ hours

Ingredients

1.5kg (3lb 5oz) braising beef, such as 900g (2lb) brisket and 600g (1lb 5oz) chuck steak

1.8kg (4lb) carrots

18 French grey shallots *(griselles)*

200g (7oz) pork belly

180g (6¼oz) butter

2 tablespoons oil

500ml (18fl oz) good-quality full-bodied red wine

100ml (3½fl oz) Cognac

1 bouquet garni

1 calf's foot, blanched, split in half and boned, bone reserved

salt and freshly ground black pepper

The French name for this recipe comes from the Poitevin-Saintongeais dialect that is spoken midway down the western coast of France and it is the local version of a traditional Provençal beef daube. Small grey shallots, also known as *griselles*, are considered to be 'true' shallots, as they can only be grown from bulbs. Compared to onions, they have quite a sweet flavour and pinkish white flesh.

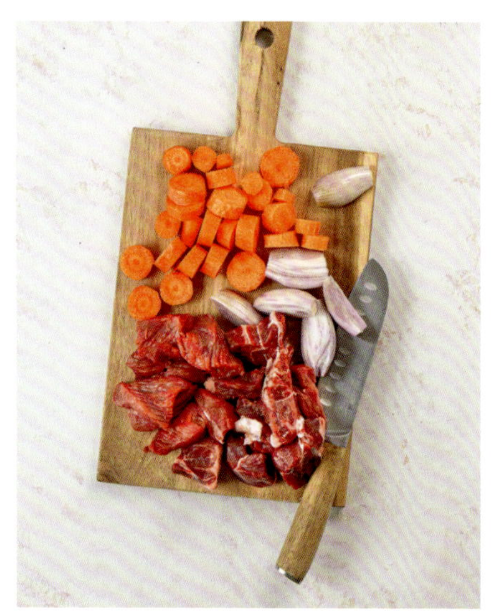

1 Cut the beef into 4cm (1½-inch) cubes. Slice the carrots into rounds and cut the shallots in half lengthways.

2 Cut the pork belly into lardons. Add the lardons to a pan of cold water, bring to the boil and blanch for 5 minutes. Drain.

3 Heat 50g (1¾oz) of the butter and the oil in a flameproof casserole over a medium heat and fry the cubes of beef until browned all over. Drain them from the casserole with a slotted spoon or skimmer and set aside.

4 Add 80g (3oz) of the butter to the casserole and gently cook the carrots for a few minutes until softened. Remove them from the pan. Add the remaining butter and fry the blanched lardons and the shallots until golden.

5 Meanwhile, heat the wine in a saucepan. Once it is hot, add the Cognac and flambé (set alight briefly) for a few minutes.

6 When the shallots are nicely golden, return the carrots and beef to the casserole. Season with salt and pepper and add the bouquet garni. Cut the flesh from the calf's foot into small dice and add with the reserved bone wrapped in a muslin bag.

7 Pour in the wine and Cognac to just come up to the same height as the meat. Cover the casserole and leave to simmer over a very low heat for at least 3 hours. The daube can also be cooked in the oven preheated to 120°C (250°F), Gas Mark ½, for 4 hours but it is advisable to make a tight seal between the pot and lid with a flour and water dough (see page 18).

8 Before serving, remove the bouquet garni and the muslin bag containing the calf's foot bone.

Tip

This dish tastes even better when it is cooked the day before and reheated.

Bordeaux-style Barbecued Entrecote Steaks

ENTRECÔTES GRILLÉES BORDELAISES

Serves 4

Preparation time: 30 mins

Cooking time: 8 mins

Resting time: 8 mins

Ingredients

2 prime entrecôte steaks, weighing 400g (14oz) each

7 or 8 grey shallots (*griselles*), roughly chopped

4 or 5 flat leaf parsley sprigs, finely chopped

salt and freshly ground black pepper

The entrecôte is a boneless beef steak cut from the rib. In English it is also known as a rib-eye and is tender, juicy and full of flavour due to the fine marbling of fat that runs through it. If you have a grapevine growing in your garden, add the branches you remove when pruning it to add flavour when barbecuing the steaks (or ask a local winemaker if they could spare you some).

1. Take the steaks out of the refrigerator about 1 hour before cooking them. Light a charcoal barbecue (or make an open fire of grapevine shoots, if available) 20–30 minutes ahead, as this will be the time needed to get a good bed of embers.

2. Place the steaks on the barbecue rack (if using an open fire, lay a grill rack over the embers and, once hot, place the steaks on the rack) just above the embers and cook for 2 minutes on each side. Season with salt and pepper.

3. Move the steaks to the side of the rack so that they cook more slowly over the less fierce heat and cook for another 2 minutes. Turn the steaks over, sprinkle over the shallots and parsley and leave to cook for another 2 minutes.

4. Transfer the steaks to a serving plate and leave them to rest for 4–5 minutes before cutting in two. Accompany with sautéed potatoes or chips.

Pauillac Roast Leg of Lamb

GIGOT D'AGNEAU DE PAUILLAC

Serves 6

Preparation time: 15 mins

Cooking time: 35–40 mins

Resting time: 10–20 mins

Ingredients

1 leg of lamb, preferably milk-fed, weighing about 1.5kg (3lb 5oz)

lamb trimmings and chump (rump) bone, roughly chopped

½ garlic bulb (cut horizontally from a whole bulb)

1 bouquet garni

salt and freshly ground black pepper

For the persillade crust

100g (3½oz) fresh breadcrumbs

2 tablespoons chopped flat leaf parsley

2 garlic cloves, chopped

The persillade breadcrumb mixture forms a beautifully golden and aromatic crust for the (preferably) milk-fed leg of lamb. Pauillac is a small town in the Haut-Médoc region of the Gironde department.

1 Preheat the oven to 220°C (425°F), Gas Mark 7. Place the leg of lamb in a roasting tin with the lamb trimmings and bone, the garlic bulb half and the bouquet garni. Season with salt and pepper. Roast for 25–30 minutes, turning the lamb over several times so that it browns evenly and basting it regularly.

2 Meanwhile, make the persillade crust. Soak the breadcrumbs briefly in water, then drain and squeeze out all the excess water. Mix the parsley and garlic with the breadcrumbs until evenly combined, then season with salt and pepper. Chill in the refrigerator until needed.

3 At the end of the roasting time for the lamb, remove it from the oven, wrap in a sheet of foil and leave it to rest for 10–20 minutes.

4 Put the roasting tin on the hob. Deglaze the pan with 300ml (10fl oz) water and stir to incorporate the juices sticking to the bottom of it. Lower the heat and let the liquid reduce by half. Strain through a conical sieve, taste and adjust the seasoning if necessary. Pour the gravy into a gravy boat and keep warm.

5 Preheat the oven grill. Press the breadcrumb and parsley mixture over the surface of the lamb with your hand. Place it under the grill and leave the persillade to colour until it becomes a beautifully golden crust.

6 Serve this very fragrant lamb with green beans or sauté potatoes.

Mussel Farmer's Mackerel

MAQUEREAUX DU BOUCHOLEUR

Serves 6 | **Preparation time: 30 mins** | **Cooking time: 20 mins**

Ingredients

1.5kg (3lb 5oz) mussels (preferably Bouchot)

6 mackerel, weighing about 300g (10½oz) each, cleaned and gutted

3 tablespoons chopped mixed herbs, such as parsley, chives and chervil

2 garlic cloves, finely chopped

100g (3½oz) white breadcrumbs

3 tablespoons olive oil

2 tablespoons white wine vinegar

lemon wedges, for squeezing over

salt and freshly ground black pepper

***Boucholeurs* is the name given to the Bouchot mussel farmers at the small, calm beach in the Charente-Maritime where the shellfish are raised (see page 47). At low tide, both the mussel beds and the farmers working them can be spotted.**

1 To prepare the mussels, pull away the thread-like 'beards' attached to the shells and scrape the shells under cold water with a small knife to remove any barnacles. Avoid soaking the mussels in cold water, as this will make them open. If any have opened, tap the shells gently and they should close again. If not, discard them, along with any mussels that have cracked or broken shells.

2 Put the mussels in a large, lidded pan, cover and cook over a high heat until all the shells have opened, shaking the pan from time to time. Discard any that remain tightly closed. Strain the cooking juices into a small casserole, remove the shells and set aside the mussel flesh.

3 Preheat the oven grill. Rinse and wipe the mackerel dry. Season them with salt and pepper and then grill them for 8–10 minutes, depending on how thick they are, turning the mackerel over carefully during the cooking time.

4 Meanwhile, add the herbs and garlic to the mussel cooking liquid and bring to the boil over a low heat. Add the breadcrumbs, followed by the mussel flesh and cook for just enough time to reheat them.

5 Lay the mackerel side by side in a hot shallow serving dish and pour over the cooking liquid. Drizzle with the oil and vinegar and serve immediately with lemon wedges for squeezing over.

Tip

Grilling is definitely the best way to cook mackerel's slightly oily flesh, but choose medium-sized line-caught fish (weighing 250–300g/9–10½oz each) rather than small mackerel. The latter, known as *lisettes*, are young fish weighing between 50–100g (1¾–3½oz), and are best kept for a recipe containing white wine.

Green Garlic Omelette

OMELETTE À L'AILLET

Serves 2 | **Preparation time: 10 mins** | **Cooking time: 10 mins**

Ingredients

6 or 7 green garlic stems

2 tablespoons olive oil

6 eggs

1 small bunch of parsley, chopped, plus extra to garnish

salt and freshly ground black pepper

Green garlic, known as *aillet* in France, is immature garlic and its appearance on market stalls is a sign that spring has arrived. Resembling a small leek, it has a soft green stem and, during Easter and Whitsun, it is traditional in the Bordeaux region to add this young garlic to an omelette.

1 As the green garlic stems are like young leeks, they will require little if any peeling. It will be sufficient to remove just the outer layer before slicing the stems crossways into small rounds.

2 Heat the oil in a frying pan, add the sliced green garlic and fry over a low heat until softened but not browned.

3 Lightly beat the eggs to break up the yolks. Season with salt and pepper and add the parsley.

4 When the fried green garlic is transparent, turn up the heat under the pan a little and pour in the egg. Cook the omelette over a medium heat, gradually drawing the egg from the edges of the pan to the middle as it sets. Shake the pan to prevent the omelette sticking to it. If you want the omelette to be *baveuse* (still runny in the centre), remove from the heat as soon as there is no more liquid.

5 Scatter more chopped parsley over the omelette as a garnish. Slide it out of the pan on to a plate without folding the omelette in half but bringing one-third to the centre and then rolling it up. Cut in half and serve with green salad or hunks of bread.

Buttered Cabbage

EMBEURRÉE DE CHOU

Serves 4–6

Preparation time: 10 mins

Cooking time: 25–35 mins

Ingredients

1 small green cabbage

100g (3½oz) butter, preferably lightly salted, cut into pieces

salt and coarsely ground black pepper

This buttered cabbage recipe also works very well if made with kale or another type of round cabbage. A few chopped chives can also be added immediately before serving.

1 Bring a large saucepan of salted water to the boil. Discard the outer leaves of the cabbage. Remove all the remaining leaves and cut away the thicker ribs. Wash the leaves thoroughly.

2 Drop the leaves into the pan of boiling water and leave them to cook, without covering the pan, for 20–30 minutes until they are very tender.

3 Cut the butter into pieces. Drain the cabbage in a colander and then press down on the leaves to remove as much water as possible. Put the cabbage back in the pan and, off the heat, crush the leaves with a fork, gradually adding some of the butter. Season with coarsely ground black pepper but only add salt if you are using unsalted butter.

4 Place the saucepan over a very low heat, add the remaining the butter and mix well. Taste and adjust the seasoning if necessary. Transfer the cabbage to a hot dish to serve.

Bordeaux-style Ceps

CÈPES À LA BORDELAISE

Serves 4

Preparation time: 30 mins

Cooking time: 10 mins

Ingredients

800g (1lb 12oz) ceps

2 tablespoons chopped parsley

2 shallots, chopped

100ml (3½fl oz) olive oil, plus an extra drizzle

juice of ½ lemon

50g (1¾oz) sandwich bread

salt and freshly ground black pepper

As ceps are porous, they must never be washed or immersed in water. Wipe them carefully, one at a time, with a damp cloth or kitchen paper and then cut away the earthy part of the stem. If the edges of a cap are shrivelled and brown, or if the underside of the cap is green, cut these parts away. Preferably choose young ceps, which are smaller.

1 Clean the ceps thoroughly with a clean cloth or kitchen paper, without washing them. Slice them if they are very large, cut them in half from top to bottom if they are medium-sized or leave them whole if they are small.

2 Mix 1 tablespoon of the chopped parsley with the shallots and set the rest aside.

3 Heat the 100ml (3½fl oz) oil in a sauté pan and add the ceps. Add the lemon juice, season with salt and pepper and cover the pan. Leave to cook for 5 minutes, stirring from time to time. Drain the ceps on to a plate lined with kitchen paper, and wipe out the pan.

4 Heat a drizzle of oil in the pan. Add the ceps and the shallots, season with salt and pepper and sauté over a brisk heat for 2–3 minutes. Break the bread into small pieces and add to the pan.

5 Drain the cep mixture from the pan, then sprinkle with the remaining parsley, mix well and serve immediately.

TAKE A STROLL
THROUGH THE FOREST...

...To Gather Mushrooms

Have you ever managed to get a dedicated mushroom forager to reveal exactly where they pick their wild mushrooms? Even for the most persuasive person, it's practically mission impossible, so why not discover your own patch by taking a stroll through a forested area. The Limousin, for example, has the ideal conditions for mushrooms to grow with its 550,000 hectares (1.35 million acres) of forests that are a mix of different types of trees (oaks, chestnuts, spruces) and its mild climate. Here you will discover a large number of different varieties of mushroom that, depending on the season, range from truffles and morels to girolles, ceps or *pied-de-mouton*. Take care, however, not to let the professional mushroom pickers beat you to it, as many people in this region of France go hunting early in the morning so that the mushrooms they gather can be shipped daily throughout Europe. Most importantly, be on your guard against 'false friends' – toxic mushrooms that look very much like the edible ones!

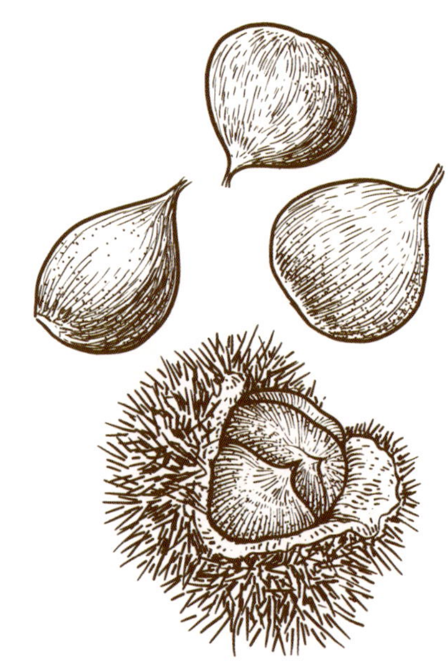

...To Discover Corsican Chestnuts

Chestnut trees grow prolifically in Corsica where they take pride of place and have been known as the 'bread trees' (*arbres à pain*) of the so-called Island of Beauty for more than 10,000 years. We tend to think of chestnuts as simply being roasted on street corners during the winter months and eaten from a paper cone, but there are multiple ways of preparing them – in fact, 28 ways, as they will tell you in Corsica. Ground to a flour, chestnuts are used in numerous recipes for baked custards, doughnuts, cakes and breads, but they can also be made into jam, a liqueur and even beer. Far from delighting only human taste buds, chestnuts are also a delicacy for the wild boar that live in the *maquis* (evergreen scrub), with the added advantage that they give the boar's meat a distinctive flavour that is *deliziosu!*

...To Hunt Game

Hunting was long a privilege reserved for the nobility and clergy, but in France it has gained in popularity over the centuries. Today it is an activity that is accessible to all with 89 species governed by legislation that can be legally hunted. The forests of the Ardennes and the Grande Sologne are two areas particularly renowned for their abundance of game of all types, including hare, pheasant, thrush, partridge, deer and, of course, the famous wild boar. Some traditions are still followed in Sologne, where deer and wild boar are hunted with hounds. Apart from being purely a hobby, hunting is also a way to regulate the numbers of certain species, such as deer, whose population has quadrupled in the space of 20 years.

...On the Trail of Red Fruits

One of summer's greatest pleasures is gathering red fruits in the undergrowth. They can be found in most forests in France from July to September. Whether you are on your own or with family members or friends, foraging in the wild offers an opportunity both to enjoy nature and make the most of berries that are rich in antioxidants and vitamins. Make jams, tarts and fruit compotes when you get back from your walk to prolong those moments of conviviality and indulgence. Remember at all times to respect the upper limit of foraging – 5kg (11lb) fruit per person in public forests – and it is a good idea to wash fruit before you eat it. Finally, respect the plants and ensure good regrowth by directly cutting the stems to collect the fruit in clusters or bunches with care.

...To Search for Wild Garlic

You can find this aromatic wild herb in alpine areas, in the undergrowth and in the forests of oak and beech trees, notably in the south-east and the Grand Est regions of north-east France. Although it grows prolifically, the picking season is quite short, extending only from February to April. It's highly sought-after, so don't hibernate for too long if you want to make the most of it. Its characteristic flavour of mild garlic and pepper combines beautifully with a salad of baby green leaves and it is delicious mixed into a pesto with ground almonds and grated Parmesan cheese.

Maraîchin Custard Tart

FLAN MARAÎCHIN

Serves 8

Preparation time: 40 mins

Resting time: 1 hour

Cooking time: 50 mins

Ingredients

For the pastry

400g (14oz) plain flour, plus extra for dusting

pinch of salt

2 eggs, beaten

150g (5½oz) butter, cut into small pieces and softened

For the filling

1 litre (1¾ pints) milk

1 vanilla pod

1 cinnamon stick

250g (9oz) sugar

9 eggs

150ml (5fl oz) full-fat crème fraîche

This custard tart, known locally in the Vendée department and the Pays de la Loire region as a *flan maraîchin* or *fion*, is the pride of the small town of Le Poiré-sur-Vie.

1 First make the pastry. Sift the flour on to the work surface, make a well in the centre and add the salt, eggs and butter. Then add 120ml (4fl oz) of cold water and mix the ingredients together with your fingertips to make a smooth dough. Shape the dough into a ball, cover with greaseproof paper and leave to rest in a cool place for 1 hour.

2 Preheat the oven to 180°C (350°F), Gas Mark 4. Roll out the pastry on a lightly floured work surface into a circle 3mm (⅛ inch) thick and use it to line a deep 25cm (10-inch) round flan tin. Prick the pastry base all over with a fork and line with nonstick baking paper. Fill with baking beans and bake blind for 15 minutes, removing the paper and beans for the final 5 minutes.

3 Meanwhile, prepare the filling. Pour the milk into a saucepan. Slit the vanilla pod lengthways in half and scrape out the seeds with the point of the knife into the milk. Add the cinnamon stick and sugar and bring to the boil. Remove from the heat and leave to infuse for about 10 minutes.

4 Beat the eggs with the crème fraîche and whisk this mixture into the infused milk, off the heat. Remove the cinnamon stick and strain through a sieve.

5 Pour the custard mixture into the pastry case and bake for 35 minutes. Remove from the oven and leave the tart to cool in the tin. Remove the tart from the tin before serving.

Île d'Yeu Prune Tart

TARTE AUX PRUNEAUX DE L'ÎLE D'YEU

Serves 4–5

Preparation time: 1 hour

Soaking time: 12 hours

Resting time: 30 mins

Cooking time: 1½ hours

Ingredients

250g (9oz) large prunes, unpitted

2 pinches of ground cinnamon

300ml (10fl oz) water

200ml (7fl oz) red wine

200g (7oz) sugar

3 tablespoons rum

For the pastry

250g (9oz) plain flour, plus extra for dusting

30g (1oz) lard, cut into small pieces

pinch of salt

125g (4oz) lightly salted butter, cold but not hard

1 egg

2 tablespoons milk

This tart is a speciality of the tiny Île d'Yeu, the furthermost island off the west coast of France. It was originally made to celebrate weddings, a tradition that still continues today.

1 The day before, soak the prunes with the cinnamon in the water and wine in a saucepan overnight or for 12 hours.

2 The next day, simmer the prunes for 1 hour in their soaking liquid. Remove from the pan (retain the soaking liquid) and, once cool, remove the stones. Return to the pan and add the sugar, rum and reserved soaking liquid. Mix well and then purée in a blender.

3 Prepare the pastry. Mix together the flour, lard, salt and 100ml (3½fl oz) of cold water in a mixing bowl to make a dough. Cover the dough with greaseproof paper and leave it to rest for 30 minutes.

4 Cut the butter into four thin slabs of equal thickness. Roll out the dough on a lightly floured work surface into a rectangle. With one short side of the rectangle towards you, place 2 slabs of the butter in the centre third of the dough, then fold the top third down to cover the butter. Place the remaining 2 slabs of butter onto the fold and then fold the bottom third of the dough up to enclose the butter completely. Give the dough a quarter turn and then roll it out into a rectangle once more. Fold and turn the dough several more times.

5 Preheat the oven to 200°C (400°F), Gas Mark 6. Roll out the dough on a lightly floured work surface and use it to line a 25cm (10-inch) round flan tin, leaving a wide border overhanging the sides of the tin. Fold this border over on to itself to make a neat edge, trimming as necessary. Reserve the trimmings.

6 Place a baking sheet in the oven, and once hot, stand the tart case on it. Bake for 7–10 minutes until the pastry is lightly golden. Reduce the oven temperature to 180°C (350°F), Gas Mark 4. Remove the tart case from the oven.

7 Fill the pastry case with the prune mixture. Layer the pastry trimmings on top of each other, roll them out thinly and cut 4 strips 1cm (½ inch) wide using a serrated pastry wheel. Beat the egg with the milk, brush it over the pastry strips to glaze them and lift 2 of the strips on to the tart, arranging them to form a 'V' pattern. Press the ends of the strips to the pastry border to fix them in place. Repeat with the remaining 2 strips, using them to form an inverted 'V' that crosses the first 2 strips. Return the tart to the oven and bake for another 20 minutes. Serve warm.

Fluted Canelé Cakes

CANNELÉS

Makes 12

Preparation time: 25 mins

Infusing time: 15 mins

Cooking time: 50 mins

Ingredients

500ml (18fl oz) milk

1 vanilla pod

2 eggs

2 egg yolks

250g (9oz) icing sugar

50g (1¾oz) butter, melted and cooled, plus extra for greasing

1 tablespoon orange flower water

100g (3½oz) plain flour

These little cakes, traditionally baked in special fluted moulds, are a speciality of Bordeaux. They caramelize on the outside but stay soft and chewy in the centre.

1 Pour the milk into a saucepan. Slit the vanilla pod lengthways in half, scrape out the seeds with the point of the knife into the milk and add the pod. Bring to the boil, then remove from the heat, cover the pan and leave the milk to infuse for 15 minutes.

2 Preheat the oven to 200°C (400°F), Gas Mark 6. Whisk the whole eggs and egg yolks with the icing sugar in a large mixing bowl until the mixture whitens. Add the melted butter and orange flower water, fold in the flour and finally mix in the vanilla-infused milk.

3 Brush 12 small dariole moulds (preferably fluted canelé moulds) with melted butter and stand them on a baking sheet. Three-quarters fill the moulds with the cake batter. Bake for about 45 minutes.

4 Unmould the canelés as soon as they come out of the oven and allow to cool completely. They are best eaten on the day they are made.

The Loire Valley

AND CENTRAL FRANCE

Sainte-Maure Cheese Puffs

FEUILLETÉS AU SAINTE-MAURE

Makes 6

Preparation time: 30 mins

Cooking time: 10 mins

Ingredients

1 Sainte-Maure de Touraine goats' cheese
200ml (7fl oz) crème fraîche
400g (14oz) ready-rolled puff pastry
1 egg
1 tablespoon milk
knob of butter, softened, for greasing
salt and freshly ground black pepper

Named after a small town in the province of Touraine, Sainte-Maure is a white, log-shaped goats' cheese that is coated in ash before being ripened. Richly flavoured, it has a creamy texture and melts in the mouth.

1. Mash the goats' cheese in a mixing bowl with a fork. Add the crème fraîche and stir until the ingredients are evenly combined and the mixture is smooth. Season with salt and pepper.
2. Lay the puff pastry sheet on the work surface and cut out 12 circles using an 8cm (3½-inch) pastry cutter. Preheat the oven to 220°C (425°F), Gas Mark 7.
3. Place 1 tablespoon of the cheese mixture in the centre of half the pastry circles. Dampen the pastry edges by brushing lightly with water and cover the filling with the remaining pastry circles, pressing the edges together to seal them tightly. Beat the egg and milk together and brush over the pastry to glaze.
4. Grease a baking sheet with the butter and place the cheese puffs on it. Bake for about 10 minutes or until they are golden brown. Serve immediately.

Asparagus Soup

POTAGE D'ASPERGES

Serves 6

Preparation time: 30 mins

Cooking time: 40 mins

Ingredients

1kg (2lb 4oz) green asparagus spears

50g (1¾oz) butter

50g (1¾oz) plain flour

500ml (18fl oz) milk

2 egg yolks

3 tablespoons crème fraîche, plus extra for serving

1 small bunch of chervil, chopped, to garnish (optional)

salt and freshly ground black pepper

This is the perfect starter for spring when asparagus is in season. In France, white asparagus is very popular and widely available, but green is used in this recipe, as it gives the soup an attractive and vibrant colour.

1 Peel the asparagus and snap or cut off the tough, most fibrous part at the end of each spear. Wash the spears and then cook them for about 20 minutes in a saucepan of salted boiling water or until tender when pierced with the tip of a sharp knife. Drain the asparagus, reserving the cooking water.

2 Cut off the tips of 6 of the asparagus spears and cut lengthways in half. Set them aside to garnish the soup.

3 Melt the butter in a heavy-based saucepan and stir in the flour until smooth. Cook until the roux turns pale golden, stirring continuously with a wooden spoon. Add 1 litre (1¾ pints) of the reserved asparagus cooking water and all the milk. Season with salt and pepper. Add the asparagus stems (but not the tips reserved for garnish) and simmer for 10 minutes.

4 Pass the soup through a food mill or purée in a blender and pour back into the saucepan to reheat. Meanwhile, whisk the egg yolks and crème fraîche together and add to the soup. Check the seasoning and sprinkle with the chopped chervil, if using. Reheat the soup over a very low heat without letting it boil. Serve immediately, swirled with a little extra crème fraîche and topped with the reserved halved asparagus tips.

Cheesy Choux Buns

GOUGÈRES

Makes 40 buns

Preparation time: 30 mins

Cooking time: 30–35 mins

Ingredients

150ml (5fl oz) milk

170g (6oz) butter

½ teaspoon salt

240g (8½oz) plain flour

6 or 7 eggs (depending on size)

150g (5½oz) Emmental or Comté cheese, grated

1 egg, beaten, to glaze

freshly ground black pepper

Serve these golden, fluffy cheese buns with pre-dinner aperitifs or as party finger food. You can make them ahead and reheat them in a hot oven for 5–10 minutes, which will also re-crisp any that have softened.

1 Put the milk, 200ml (7fl oz) water, the butter and salt in a saucepan and bring to the boil. Remove the pan from the heat, add the flour all in one go and stir briskly until evenly mixed in and smooth. Return the pan to a low heat and cook for 2–3 minutes, stirring continuously with a wooden spoon to dry out the mixture sufficiently for it to come away from the sides of the pan.

2 Take the pan off the heat and beat in the eggs, one at a time, ensuring that each egg is completely incorporated before adding the next. The paste must not be too soft, so if it starts to become wet, do not add the final egg. Once the eggs have been beaten in, stir in the grated cheese and season with pepper.

3 Preheat the oven to 180°C (350°F), Gas Mark 4. Line 1 large or 2 smaller baking sheets with nonstick baking paper. Transfer the choux paste to a piping bag fitted with a large plain nozzle and pipe about 40 small choux buns on to the lined baking sheets. Brush the buns with the beaten egg to glaze and bake for 25–30 minutes or until they are puffed and golden brown. Serve warm.

Snails Stuffed with Garlic Butter

ESCARGOTS À LA BOURGUIGNONNE

Serves 4–8

Preparation time: 40 mins

Cooking time: 10 mins

Ingredients

48 canned snails (with their shells separate)

15g (½oz) garlic, chopped

25g (1oz) shallots, chopped

15g (½oz) flat leaf parsley, chopped

150g (5½oz) fresh butter, softened, plus extra for the shells

salt and freshly ground black pepper

Snails have long been a gourmet delicacy in France, as shells discovered on archaeological digs prove they have been eaten in the country since prehistoric times. Later, they were enjoyed by the Romans and Greeks, and in the Middle Ages snails were bred in convents to ensure there was food during times of famine. Burgundy snails are large, with brown and white striped shells and are prized throughout France for their flavour. Canned snails are available to buy online, in larger supermarkets and in specialist stores.

1 Rinse the snails and dry them on kitchen paper.

2 Mix the garlic, shallots and parsley with the butter. Season lightly with salt and more generously with pepper and then mash with a fork or a pestle until evenly mixed.

3 Slide a small knob of butter into each snail shell, pushing it right to the bottom, then place a snail in each and finish by filling the shells with the garlic butter. Sit the filled shells in the hollows of individual snail serving dishes or carefully pack in heatproof bowls or a gratin dish, ensuring the opening of each shell is uppermost.

4 Preheat the oven grill. When it is very hot, slide the dishes of snails under the grill and remove them after about 10 minutes, by which time the butter will be bubbling. Serve immediately.

Tip

You can buy individual snail serving dishes, either metal or ceramic, if you want to get serious about eating snails.

Fresh Goats' Cheese with Garlic and Herbs

CLAQUEBITOU

Serves 4

Preparation time: 10 mins

Chilling time: 2 hours

Ingredients

500g (1lb 2oz) fresh goats' cheese

1 tablespoon white wine vinegar

1 or 2 garlic cloves, crushed

4 shallots, very finely chopped, plus extra to garnish

1 small bunch of chives, chopped, plus extra to garnish and to serve

1 small bunch of flat leaf parsley, chopped

salt and freshly ground black pepper

crème fraîche, to serve

Claquebitou is the name given in the Charolais region of Burgundy to this farmhouse goats' cheese mixed with garlic and herbs. Soft in texture, the cheese has a woody flavour and is in season during the spring, summer and autumn months. Serve it as a starter or as part of a cheese board.

1. Put the cheese in a mixing bowl, add the vinegar and whisk lightly. Add the garlic, shallots and herbs and mix together. Season with salt and pepper.
2. Chill in the refrigerator for a minimum of 2 hours.
3. Serve the cheese sprinkled with extra chopped shallots and chives to garnish, accompanied with a bowl of crème fraîche and a separate bowl of chopped chives for garnishing according to your preference.

Tip

Claquebitou should not be confused with Clacbitou, which is the brand name of a quite different style of cheese.

CHABICHOU, PÉLARDON
& COMPANY

Chabichou, How Cute are You!

In addition to winning the trophy for the cutest cheese name in France, Chabichou du Poitou could legitimately claim to be taken seriously when it was granted AOC status in 1990. Shaped like a small cylinder called a *bonde* (the bung of a wine barrel), this goats' cheese is also very stylish. Its fine white crust tinged with grey can sometimes be covered with light red and yellow dots and it is adorned with a traditional medallion-shaped label with small straps. Its terroir is also very precise, being limited to one part of the departments of Vienne, Deux-Sèvres and the Charente.

Rocamadour Amour

This small raw milk cheese comes from the town of the same name in the Lot department and has been known to fine food lovers since at least the 15th century. Its reputation led to it being granted well-deserved AOC status in 1996. When fresh, Rocamadour releases creamy flavours with a mild goat-like aroma that become stronger as it ages and the cheese becomes drier.

Pélardon is the G.o.a.t.

Contrary to what you might think from its name, Pélardon is not a special kind of charcuterie but a small goats' cheese made in the Cévennes region. It is also one of the oldest goats' cheeses in Europe. Made in the Languedoc, it is produced from fresh milk curd that is ladled into moulds the same day and then ripened for about ten days. This traditional manufacturing process earned it AOP (Protected Designation of Origin) certification in 2001. Appreciated for its smoothness and characteristic taste, it is enjoyed both cold and hot, accompanied with honey or jam, but always with a good slice of artisan bread!

Roquefort Rocks It

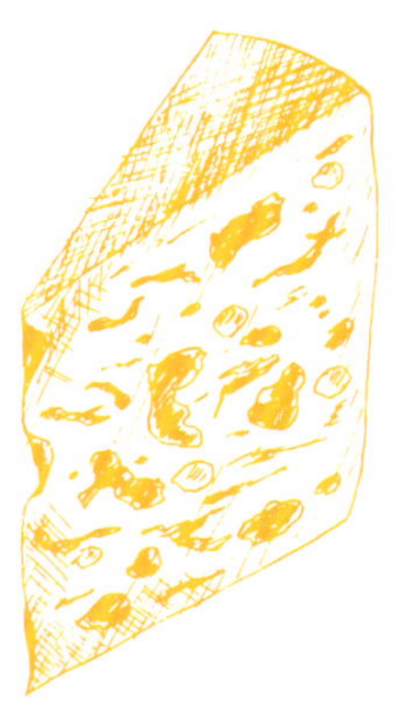

Internationally known, Roquefort is the oldest star in the French cheese galaxy, being the first to be granted AOC certification a century ago. Produced from sheep's milk – unlike its blue cousin, Bleu des Causses AOC, which is made from cows' milk – it is recognizable by its cylindrical shape and blue veining. This distinctive colour is due to the curd being inoculated with *Penicillium roqueforti*, an edible mould that develops as the cheese ripens in caves dug out of the limestone scree in the region of Rouergue and Causses.

To You Brocciu, Bon Appettitu! (As They Say in Corsica)

If we could only keep one Corsican cheese, it would have to be Brocciu. Holding AOC certification, it is made from the whey of sheep's and goats' milk, dairy cows being very rare in Corsica. Two styles of the cheese are produced: soft with no crust when it has not been ripened, and dry and salty (Brocciu Passu) after 15 days of ripening. Serve the cheese accompanied with chestnut jam or Corsican honey to enjoy it at its best or add it to the famous *fiadone*, a type of lemon-flavoured cheesecake that is traditionally made on the so-called Island of Beauty (see recipe page 300). And to ensure you do not reveal yourself as a *pinzutu*, a foreigner from mainland Europe, take care to pronounce its name correctly: 'Brotchiou'.

A Merry Berry Paradise... for Goats' Cheese!

The region of Berry, in Centre, is extremely prolific in terms of goats' cheese production, the most famous of which all benefit from AOC certification. In the Sancerre region, you can enjoy a delicious Crottin de Chavignol, which pairs perfectly with many of the Sancerre wines that are another speciality of the area. To the west of the River Indre, it is Pouligny-Saint-Pierre, a small, white, pyramid-shaped cheese, that will satisfy your taste buds. Selles-sur-Cher, which is distinctive due to its ash covering, is from a particular area that straddles Berry, Sologne and Touraine, while Valençay, shaped like a small, truncated pyramid with a bluish crust, is found to the north of Châteauroux. First the wine route, then the cheese route!

Eggs Poached in Red Wine Sauce

OEUFS EN MEURETTE

Serves 4

Preparation time: 1 hour

Cooking time: 25 mins

Ingredients

200g (7oz) lightly salted back bacon, rinded and cut into small dice

100g (3½oz) onions or shallots, finely chopped

60g (2½oz) butter

1 bouquet garni

1 bottle of Burgundy red wine

250ml (9fl oz) very concentrated beef stock

8 small thin slices of bread

2 garlic cloves, peeled

1 bottle of red table wine or 750ml (1⅓ pints) water

50ml (2fl oz) red wine vinegar

8 eggs

salt and freshly ground black pepper

chopped flat leaf parsley, to garnish

A classic in Burgundian cuisine, this dish is similar to beef bourguignon (see page 138) but poached eggs rather than beef are served in a red wine sauce. This *meurette* sauce is even better when reheated, so it can be prepared in advance.

1. Put the diced bacon into a saucepan of cold water, bring to the boil and cook for 2 minutes. Drain and refresh under cold running water.

2. Fry the onions or shallots in 40g (1½oz) of the butter in a large, deep frying pan over a low heat until they are transparent. Add the bacon and bouquet garni, then pour in the Burgundy wine and boil until reduced by half. Pour in the stock and again boil until reduced by half. Cut the remaining butter into small pieces and gradually whisk them in. Season with salt and pepper and keep the sauce hot.

3. Toast the slices of bread until golden brown on both sides, then briskly rub the garlic cloves over them. Place 2 slices on each of 4 hot serving plates.

4. Pour the table wine or water and vinegar into a sauté pan, season lightly with salt and pepper. Bring to the boil then lower the heat under the pan. Just before serving, break the eggs into the cooking liquid and poach them for 3 minutes.

5. Using a skimmer, carefully lift out the eggs in the order that you added them to the pan and drain them on kitchen paper. Cut off the small white threads that have formed around the eggs and lift each egg on to a slice of toasted bread. Cover with the sauce, garnish with chopped flat leaf parsley and serve immediately.

Chicken Fricassée

FRICASSÉE DE POULET

Serves 6

Preparation time: 30 mins

Cooking time: 50 mins

Ingredients

350g (12oz) small button mushrooms

juice of 1 lemon

2 tablespoons oil

1 chicken, weighing about 2kg (4lb 8oz), cut into 12 pieces

100g (3½oz) butter

24 small pearl onions, peeled

300ml (10fl oz) Anjou white wine

200ml (7fl oz) crème fraîche

salt and freshly ground black pepper

If chicken fricassée is a traditional dish in Anjou, it is in neighbouring Sarthe, around the city of Le Mans, that the best birds to make it come from – Loué chickens.

1 Wipe the mushrooms clean and trim the stems but leave them whole. Squeeze the lemon juice over them to prevent them discolouring.

2 Heat the oil in a flameproof casserole over a medium heat and fry the chicken pieces until they are golden brown. Remove the chicken and pour off the fat from the casserole. Add half the butter and gently fry the onions until they are golden. Return the chicken pieces to the casserole, pour in the wine and season with salt and pepper. Cover the casserole and leave to simmer for 40 minutes.

3 Meanwhile, heat the remaining butter in a sauté pan and fry the mushrooms over a low heat without covering the pan. When the chicken has been simmering for 20 minutes, drain the mushrooms and add them to the casserole.

4 When the chicken pieces are cooked through, lift them out of the casserole and transfer them to a serving dish and keep hot. Stir the crème fraîche into the sauce, bring it to the boil and reduce by half. Pour the sauce over the chicken in the serving dish.

Andouillettes with Vouvray

ANDOUILLETTES AU VOUVRAY

Serves 6

Preparation time: 10 mins

Cooking time: 25 mins

Ingredients

6 andouillettes

6 shallots, finely chopped

50g (1¾oz) butter, cut into small pieces

200ml (7fl oz) dry Vouvray white wine

100ml (3½floz) crème fraîche

In Touraine, any self-respecting andouillette must come *à la corde* (on a rope), meaning the pig intestines and pieces of pork belly used to make it are plaited around a rope, and the andouillette is then cooked in stock flavoured with Vouvray wine. If made in this way, which follows the artisan rules, it is certified '5' by the Association Amicale des Amateurs d'Andouillette Authentique. However, whether artisanal or industrially produced, andouillettes being grilled on charcoal embers take pride of place at all popular festivals and other big Touraine celebrations.

1. Preheat the oven to 200°C (400°F), Gas Mark 6. Put the andouillettes in a shallow baking tray and prick them before putting them in the oven.

2. Once the andouillettes have started to turn golden brown, spread out the shallots around them. Dot the butter over the shallots.

3. When the andouillettes are cooked, after about 20 minutes, remove them from the oven to serving plates and keep hot.

4. Deglaze the baking tray with the wine, boiling to reduce it by half. Whisk the crème fraîche into the sauce and then spoon it over the andouillettes. Serve hot with chips or potatoes baked in the oven.

Pork and Green Lentil Casserole

POTÉE DE LENTILLES VERTES

Serves 8

Preparation time: 40 mins

Cooking time: about 3 hours

Ingredients

1.5kg (3lb 5oz) salt pork, from the leg, ribs or knuckle (or use unsmoked gammon)

300g (10½oz) smoked pork belly

1 pig's tail

2 pig's trotters

3 cloves

2 onions

4 leeks, trimmed and cleaned

5 carrots, cut into pieces

3 turnips, cut into pieces

2 garlic cloves, peeled

1 bouquet garni

10 black peppercorns

1 small cabbage, cut into large pieces

500g (1lb 2oz) potatoes

1 French garlic poaching sausage (*saucisson à l'ail à cuire*), pricked with a fork

300g (10½oz) Berry green lentils

1 celery stick, sliced

salt and freshly ground black pepper

A *potée* is a traditional French farmhouse dish that is either a soup or a stew. Cooked in one large pot, it makes a satisfying and sustaining meal. Green lentils from Berry are recognized with the Label Rouge. The salt pork used here, known as *petit-salé* in France, is where the meat has been immersed in brine for up to two days.

1. Wash all the meats, including the pig's tail and trotters, in plenty of water. Put them in a large flameproof cooking pot and cover with fresh cold water. Bring to the boil, skimming off any foam, then cover the pot and leave the meats to cook with the water bubbling gently. Stick the cloves into the peeled onions. Tie the leeks into bundles with kitchen string.

2. After the meats have been simmering for 1½ hours, add the leeks, carrots, turnips, onions, garlic cloves, bouquet garni and peppercorns. Cook for 45 minutes and then add the cabbage, potatoes and sausage. Simmer for another 30 minutes.

3. Meanwhile, pick over the lentils and remove any small stones or other debris. Rinse them in a sieve under cold running water. Put them in a heavy-based flameproof casserole with the celery and cover completely with fresh cold water. Season with salt and pepper.

4. Cook the lentils over a very low heat for about 40 minutes until tender. The water must remain just trembling and never boil rapidly, otherwise the skins of the lentils, which are particularly fragile, might burst.

5. Arrange the meats, vegetables and lentils in a hot serving dish (you can slice the salt pork at this point, if you wish, and take out the tail and trotters). Remove any fat from the surface of the cooking juices and serve the juices in cups alongside the meat, vegetables and lentils.

Beef Bourguignon

BOEUF BOURGUIGNON

Serves 6	Preparation time: 30 mins	Marinating time: 24 hours	Cooking time: 3 hours 10 mins

200g (7oz) streaky bacon, rinded

24 pearl onions

100g (3½oz) butter

salt and freshly ground black pepper

2 tablespoons oil

400g (14oz) small button mushrooms

2 tablespoons plain flour

1.5kg (3lb 5oz) braising beef (chuck steak or shoulder)

2 or 3 shallots

2 tablespoons oil

1 bouquet garni

1 litre (1¾ pints) red wine

1 large onion

1 heaped teaspoon crushed black peppercorns

2 tablespoons marc de Bourgogne

Ingredients

1.5kg (3lb 5oz) braising beef (chuck steak or shoulder)

2 tablespoons oil

100g (3½oz) butter

2 tablespoons plain flour

400g (14oz) small button mushrooms

24 pearl onions

200g (7oz) streaky bacon, rinded

salt and freshly ground black pepper

For the marinade

2 tablespoons oil

1 litre (1¾ pints) red wine

2 tablespoons marc de Bourgogne

1 large onion, finely sliced

2 or 3 shallots, finely sliced

1 bouquet garni

1 heaped teaspoon crushed black peppercorns

1 The day before, prepare the marinade. Cut the meat into large cubes and place them in a bowl.

2 First, spoon the oil for the marinade over the meat and then pour in the wine and marc. Add the onion, shallots, bouquet garni and crushed peppercorns. Mix everything together thoroughly, cover the bowl and leave to marinate for 24 hours in the refrigerator.

3 The next day, drain the meat and pat it dry with kitchen paper. Strain the marinade through a fine sieve and set it aside.

4 Heat the 2 tablespoons of oil and 60g (2¼oz) of the butter in a flameproof casserole over a medium heat. Brown the meat for 3–4 minutes, turning the pieces several times so that they colour evenly. Remove the meat from the casserole with a slotted spoon and set aside.

5 Discard the fat in the casserole. Add 20g (¾oz) of the butter to the casserole and, once it melts, return the meat and its juices. Dust the meat with the flour and cook over a brisk heat, turning the pieces several times.

6 Bring the marinade to the boil in a saucepan and immediately pour it into the casserole. Season with salt and pepper. Cover and leave to cook gently for 2½ hours, checking the seasoning halfway through and adding more if necessary.

7 Towards the end of the cooking time, wipe the mushrooms clean and trim the stems. Peel the pearl onions.

8 Cut the bacon into lardons and fry them gently in a saucepan for 7–8 minutes so that the fat melts.

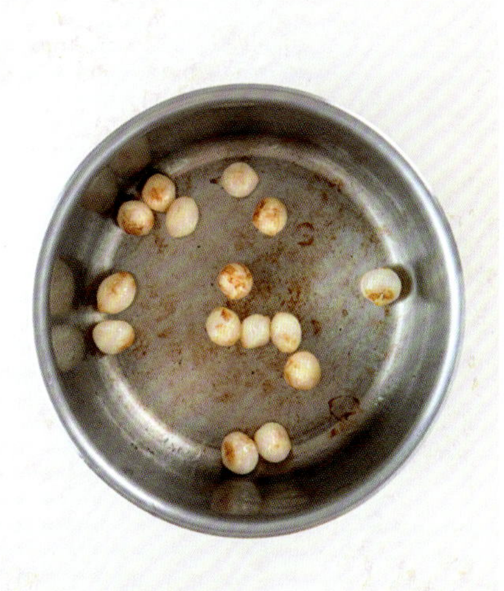

9 Remove the bacon from the pan with a skimmer and add the pearl onions. Cover the pan and cook for 10 minutes over a very low heat. Uncover and cook for a few more minutes until the onions are lightly golden. Remove them from the pan and set aside with the lardons.

10 Add the mushrooms to the saucepan with the remaining butter and fry for 5 minutes over a medium heat. Return the lardons and pearl onions to the pan.

11 Check that the meat is cooked by testing a piece with the point of a sharp knife. Once the meat is tender, remove the bouquet garni. Add the pearl onions, lardons and mushrooms to the casserole and continue to cook for another 30 minutes. Serve hot with boiled or steamed parsley potatoes.

Seven-hour Leg of Lamb

GIGOT DE SEPT HEURES

Serves 6

Preparation time: 1 hour

Cooking time: 7 hours 10 mins

Ingredients

1 leg of lamb, weighing 2.5kg–3kg (5lb 8oz–6lb 8oz)

300g (10½oz) streaky bacon rashers

100ml (3½fl oz) oil

3 carrots, sliced into rounds

300g (10½oz) pork skin or bacon rind

1 or 2 bay leaves

3 thyme sprigs

1 garlic bulb, halved horizontally, plus 6 garlic cloves, unpeeled

100ml (3½fl oz) Cognac

2 tablespoons tomato purée

2 teaspoons veal stock powder

dry white wine (optional)

salt and freshly ground black pepper

Slow-cooking a leg of lamb for seven hours in a tightly sealed casserole ensures that it will be melt-in-the-mouth tender, with meat that falls off the bone. While cooking the lamb requires no attention beyond checking the juices in the casserole, be careful not to boil it dry towards the end of the cooking time.

1 Ask your butcher to bone the leg of lamb for you, leaving only the shank bone, and to lard it with the streaky bacon. Preheat the oven to 150°C (300°F), Gas Mark 2.

2 Heat a little of the oil in a large cast-iron casserole and brown the leg of lamb on all sides. Remove it from the casserole. Add the carrots to the casserole, fry until they are golden and then remove them. Line the bottom of the casserole with the pieces of pork skin or bacon rind.

3 Return the leg of lamb to the casserole and then add the carrots, bay leaves, thyme, garlic bulb halves, garlic cloves, Cognac and tomato purée. Dissolve the veal stock powder in 500ml (18fl oz) hot water and pour into the casserole. Season with salt and pepper. Cover the casserole, making a tight seal between the pot and lid with a flour and water dough (see page 18). If the casserole has a recessed lid, pour water into this. If not, pour 2 glasses of water into a roasting tin and place this in the bottom of the oven to create a moist environment as the lamb cooks.

4 Cook the lamb in the oven for 7 hours. Check regularly that the cooking juices have not evaporated and, if necessary, top them up with dry white wine as the lamb cooks. Serve with white haricot beans or simply with potatoes cooked in the oven.

GRILL, ROAST
OR SIMMER

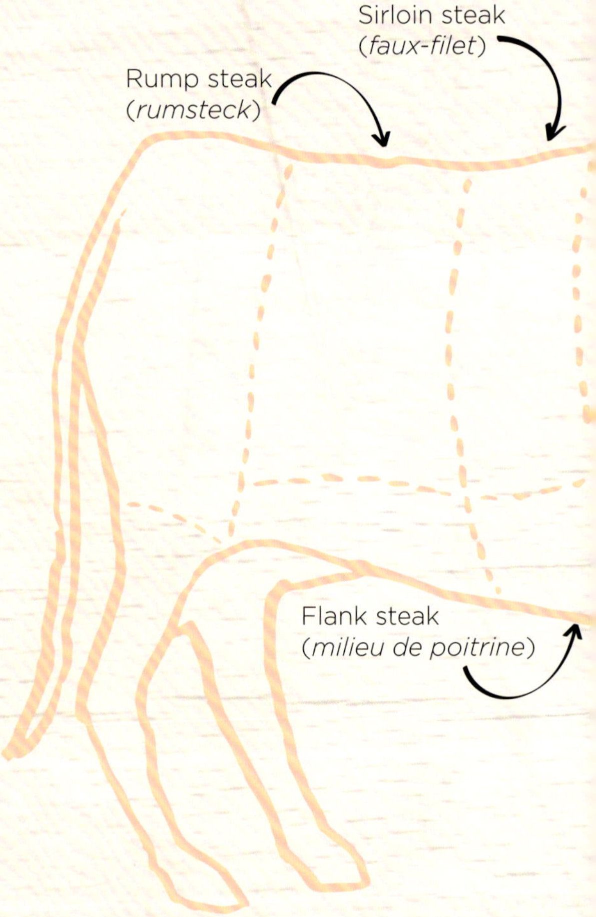

Sirloin steak
(*faux-filet*)

Rump steak
(*rumsteck*)

Flank steak
(*milieu de poitrine*)

For the Love of Limousin

First, let us talk about Limousin, a breed of cattle that has been highly prized in France since the 17th century. This resplendent beast with its fawn coat and massive head has won over red meat lovers around the world, but what makes it so special? The Limousin is a rustic breed that has been able to adapt to the rugged terrain and harsh climate of the Limousin region. Raised in the open air, the cattle are fattened on fresh grass and dried hay and they grow at their own pace, free from stress and other constraints. This is evident in the quality of their tender, juicy and flavourful meat, which lends itself to all types of cooking from *pot-au-feu* to plain grilling or, for more adventurous cooks, carpaccio and steak tartare.

No Beef with Aubrac Beef

Aubrac beef is a meat that makes the hearts of even the most demanding gourmets beat faster and has them reaching for their steak knives and forks. Living for centuries in the Aveyron mountains, this breed was originally used as a working beast to pull ploughs, since it could withstand the wide variations in temperature and walk long distances. However, today, the breed is famous above all for its meat. Raised at an altitude of more than 1,000 metres (3,280 feet), Aubrac cattle are fed on fresh meadow grass, combined with GMO-free cereal supplements. This produces meat with firm, marbled flesh that is incredibly tasty and will leave an unforgettable impression on your taste buds.

Championing Charolais

Charolais beef is by far the best-known breed of French cattle and as a result is one of the most highly appreciated in France. Native to the Charolles region in Burgundy, today the cattle are raised on farms throughout France and also in more than 70 other countries. Recognizable by their white or cream coats, the cattle are mostly raised in the traditional way of respecting the pasture-barn cycle. The breed is particularly popular with farmers for its significant growth potential and with butchers for the quality of its meat, which is low in fat and full of flavour. Since 2010, Charolles beef has benefited from being granted AOC certification, which makes it one of only four French breeds to be recognized in this way.

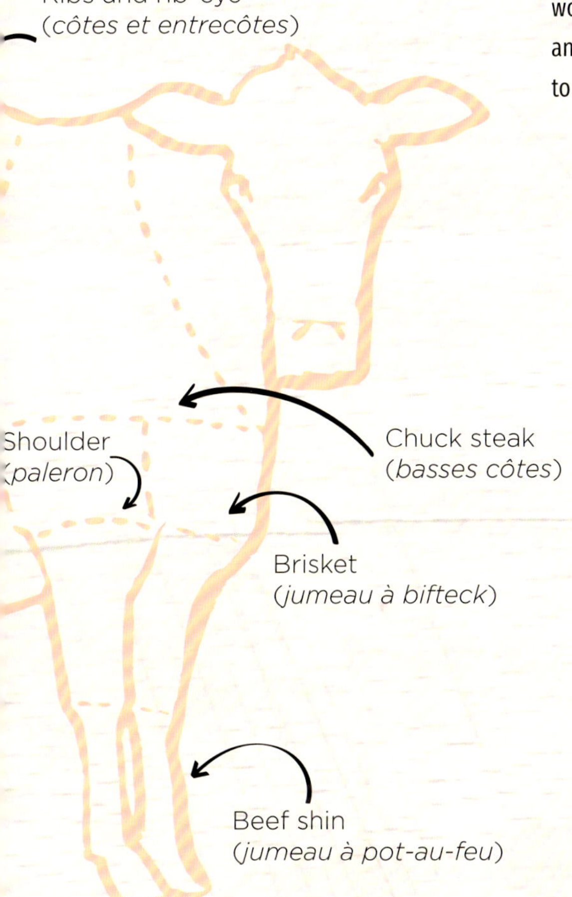

Cheers for Chalosse

Chalosse beef is a generic name grouping together several breeds of cattle that are raised in the Chalosse region south of Landes: the Limousin, the Blonde d'Aquitaine and the crossing of these two stars of the bovine world. Raised on pasture, then fattened with corn meal and hay, the animals are renowned for their well-marbled meat, which is well suited to many different recipes and dishes!

Lazing and Grazing on the Beach

This is (almost) true of the salt-marsh lambs of Mont Saint-Michel in Normandy, but minus the sun protection cream! The pastures in which they are raised are regularly flooded with water during the local high tides, which drenches the land and grass with salt and leads to the growth of several varieties of marine plants, such as marsh samphire. This addition to the animals' diet gives their meat its characteristic flavour, but care must be taken, as this rare and high-quality meat can fall victim to fraud. In season from April to December, the farms raising these lambs are obliged to carry AOC certification, which guarantees the provenance of the meat to the customer.

The Black Gold of the Basque Country, Porc Favor!

Lovers of charcuterie must not miss this culinary black gold! Also known as Basque pork, the Pie Noir of the Basque Country is a local breed of pig that lives exclusively in the mountains and forests of the French and Spanish Basque Country. A tough breed, it adapts perfectly to its natural environment, which means it can be raised solely outdoors. Alongside the usual fattening diet, it also feeds on chestnuts, acorns and roots, which give the meat a rich flavour with woody and slightly sweet notes. It is used in the manufacture of traditional charcuterie, including ham from the Aldudes valley, Bayonne ham, French-style pancetta known as *ventrèche*, Basque sausage and many more...

Rabbit with Mustard Sauce

LAPIN À LA MOUTARDE

Serves 6

Preparation time: 20 mins

Cooking time: 50 mins

Ingredients

1 rabbit, weighing about 1.5kg (3lb 5oz), with its liver

3 tablespoons oil

6 tablespoons wholegrain Dijon mustard

2 tablespoons thyme leaves

100ml (3½fl oz) dry white wine

6 tablespoons crème fraîche

salt and freshly ground black pepper

This is a traditional French recipe for rabbit flavoured with a Dijon mustard sauce. When you add the liver to the rabbit, check the consistency of the sauce. If you think it is too liquid, take the lid off the casserole before the end of the cooking time so that the sauce can thicken a little.

1 Cut the rabbit into pieces. Set aside the liver. Preheat the oven to 180°C fan (350°F), Gas Mark 4. Heat the oil in a frying pan and brown the rabbit pieces over a high heat, turning them over several times so that they colour evenly.

2 As the rabbit pieces become golden brown, remove them from the pan, coat them with the mustard and place side by side in a flameproof casserole. Season very lightly with salt (the mustard will already have added salt) and pepper and sprinkle with the thyme leaves. Cover the casserole and cook in the oven for 30 minutes.

3 Remove the casserole from the oven. Lift out the rabbit pieces, retrieving any mustard that has fallen off them as well, and place in a dish. Put the casserole on the hob over a medium heat, pour in the wine and cook for 1–2 minutes. Add the crème fraîche and bring to the boil, giving the bottom of the casserole a good scrape so that the juices sticking to it dissolve into the sauce. Taste and adjust the seasoning, if necessary.

4 Return the rabbit pieces to the casserole and add the liver. Cover the casserole and cook in the oven for another 10 minutes.

5 Arrange the rabbit pieces in a hot serving dish. Slice the liver and add it to the dish. Spoon over the sauce and serve immediately.

Zander with Vouvray

SANDRE À LA VOUVRILLONNE

Serves 6

Preparation time: 30 mins

Cooking time: 50 mins–1 hour

Ingredients

1 zander, weighing 1.5kg–2kg (3lb 5oz–4lb 8oz), scaled, gutted and filleted

300g (10½oz) oyster mushrooms

50g (1¾oz) butter

3 carrots, cut into small slices

3 celery sticks, cut into small dice

3 thyme sprigs

1 bay leaf

1 garlic clove, chopped

4 shallots, chopped

5 pearl onions, peeled

1 bottle of dry Vouvray white wine

Zander, also known as pikeperch, has quite firm, meaty flesh scented with the aromas of fresh herbs. It can grow up to 90cm (3 feet) long, and has spiny fins and sharp teeth. Brownish-green along the back, where it has two separate dorsal fins, its skin fades to white with a silvery sheen on the underside. Zander is now an invasive species in UK waters and not known in North America. Its relative the walleye (pikeperch) or trout are suitable alternatives.

1. Rinse the fish and pat dry with kitchen paper.

2. Halve the oyster mushrooms, trimming the tips of their stems if they are dried out.

3. Heat the butter in a sauté pan and sweat the carrots and celery over a gentle heat with the thyme and bay leaf. Add the mushrooms and then the garlic, shallots and pearl onions and continue cooking until the onions are golden. Preheat the oven to 200°C (400°F), Gas Mark 6.

4. Transfer the vegetables to a deep ovenproof dish. Place the fish in it, add the wine and bake for 30–40 minutes, basting the fish regularly with the wine. Once the fish has turned golden brown, lower the oven temperature to 160°C (325°F), Gas Mark 3 and cover the dish with foil for the remaining cooking time.

5. Serve the fish accompanied with steamed or boiled potatoes or with fresh pasta.

Pithivier

Serves 8 | **Preparation time: 45 mins** | **Cooking time: 45 mins**

Ingredients

700g (1lb 8oz) block of puff pastry (shop-bought or homemade)

plain flour, for dusting

250g (9oz) ground almonds

6 egg yolks

250g (9oz) sugar

8g (¼oz) sachet vanilla sugar

200g (7oz) butter, softened

3 tablespoons rum

1 egg

1 tablespoon milk

Pithiviers, a town in the Loiret department of north-central France, gives its name to one of the country's most famous sweet pastries. Similar to the *galette des rois*, which is eaten at Epiphany, pithivier is two layers of melt-in-the-mouth puff pastry that are sandwiched together with sweet rum- and vanilla-flavoured frangipane. However, it is not Pithiviers' only claim to fame, as long before the flaky pastry version was invented, the *pithiviers fondant* (melting pithivier) was the local speciality. This was an equally delicious cake, made from almonds, eggs, butter and sugar, that was iced and decorated with candied fruits.

1 Divide the puff pastry into 2 pieces, one weighing 300g (10oz) and the other 400g (14oz). Roll out each piece thinly on a lightly floured work surface into circles of the same size.

2 Make the filling. Put the ground almonds and egg yolks in a mixing bowl and stir briskly until evenly combined. Mix in the sugar and vanilla sugar until you have a smooth mixture. Finally, gradually mix in the butter and the rum.

3 Preheat the oven to 230°C (450°F), Gas Mark 8. Line a baking sheet with nonstick baking paper.

4 Carefully lift the thinner pastry circle (rolled from the larger quantity of pastry) on to the lined baking sheet. Spoon the almond filling into the centre of the pastry and spread it out in an even layer, leaving a 1.5cm (⅝-inch) border around the edge. Brush the border with water.

5 Lift the second pastry circle over the almond filling, pressing the pastry edges together all the way round to seal them. With the point of a sharp knife, scallop the outside edge of the pithivier by making a small cut in the pastry at even intervals (or use a small semicircular pastry cutter) and score diamond- or rose-shaped patterns in the pastry top. Beat the egg and milk together and brush over the pastry to glaze.

6 Bake the pithivier for 45 minutes, lowering the oven temperature to 200°C (400°F), Gas Mark 6 when the pastry top has browned sufficiently. Serve warm or cold.

Cremets d'Anjou

CRÉMETS D'ANJOU

Serves 6

Preparation time: 15 mins

Chilling/draining time: 8 hours

Ingredients

6 egg whites

pinch of salt

500ml (18fl oz) double cream, well chilled

100g (3½oz) icing sugar (plain or vanilla-flavoured), sifted, plus extra for dusting

red fruit coulis or fresh red berries, to serve

This creamy French dessert from Anjou was originally made with equal quantities of fromage blanc and crème fraîche, but this recipe combines a Chantilly cream – lightly sweetened, vanilla-flavoured whipped cream – with stiffly beaten egg whites. If you have any perforated fromage blanc containers, these can be used to make individual servings, unless you have the special heart-shaped china cremets dishes. Otherwise, yogurt pots with tiny holes punched in them, or even tiny flower pots lined with muslin, would be suitable. Alternatively, use a fine-mesh sieve to make one large cremet.

1. Whisk the egg whites with the salt in a large mixing bowl until they are standing in firm peaks.

2. Make the Chantilly cream. Pour the cream into a separate mixing bowl, then stand the bowl in another bowl filled with ice cubes. Whisking vigorously, gradually add the icing sugar, a little at a time, until it is all incorporated.

3. Gradually fold the whisked egg whites lightly into the Chantilly cream, again a little at a time, until evenly combined.

4. Line 6 individual serving containers or a fine-mesh sieve with a square of muslin or gauze. Stand the containers in a dish or, if using a fine-mesh sieve, place the sieve over a bowl. Spoon in the mixture and chill for at least 8 hours to allow it to drain well.

5. Unmould the cremets into individual bowls, or place a serving dish on top of the sieve, upturn it and peel away the muslin or gauze. Dust with icing sugar and serve with a red fruit coulis or fresh red berries.

Sablé-sur-Sarthe Sables

SABLÉS DE SABLÉ-SUR-SARTHE

Makes 50

Preparation time: 20 mins

Resting time: 30 mins

Cooking time: 10–12 mins per batch

Ingredients

200g (7oz) best-quality French unsalted butter, plus extra for greasing

100g (3½oz) icing sugar

4 egg yolks

pinch of salt

320g (11¼oz) plain flour, plus extra for dusting

120ml/4fl oz milk

You would have your work cut out to compete with the bakers and pastry chefs of Sablé, a town on the River Sarthe in the Pays de la Loire, who excel in making these irresistible shortbread-style biscuits. But don't let that put you off, as the recipe is simple to make – the secret of its success lies in using only the finest butter and the right size grain of sugar.

1. Take the butter out of the refrigerator at least 2 hours before you need it. Beat the butter with the icing sugar in a mixing bowl until light and creamy, then beat in 3 of the egg yolks and the salt. Gradually fold in the flour, followed by enough of the milk to make a smooth but not soft dough. Shape the dough into a ball, wrap it in greaseproof paper and leave it to rest for 30 minutes in the refrigerator.

2. Preheat the oven to 220°C (425°F), Gas Mark 7. Grease a baking sheet with butter. Roll out the dough on a lightly floured work surface into a large sheet about 4mm (⅛ inch) thick. Using a 6cm (2½-inch) fluted pastry cutter, cut out circles and place them on the baking sheet. Beat the last egg yolk with 3 tablespoons of milk and brush over the sables.

3. Bake the sables in batches for 10–12 minutes until they are just golden. Remove from the oven and leave them to cool on a wire rack. Once cold, the sables can be stored in an airtight container for up to 10 days.

The South West

Foie Gras Terrine

TERRINE DE FOIE GRAS MI-CUIT

Makes 1kg (2lb 4oz) terrine	Preparation time: 15 mins	Marinating time: 12 hours	Cooking time: 40 mins

1kg (2lb 4oz) duck (or goose) foie gras

16g (½oz) salt

100ml (3½fl oz) white port

5g (¼oz) freshly ground white pepper

1 teaspoon *quatre-épices*

Ingredients

1kg (2lb 4oz) duck (or goose) foie gras

16g (½oz) salt

5g (⅛oz) freshly ground white pepper

1 teaspoon *quatre-épices* (a French spice mix of ground pepper, cloves, nutmeg, ginger or cinnamon)

100ml (3½fl oz) white port

1 Separate the lobes of foie gras and remove the veins using your fingers or tweezers. Put the lobes in a shallow dish and dust them on both sides with the salt, white pepper and *quatre-épices*. Drizzle over the port and leave to marinate for 12 hours in the refrigerator, turning the lobes over 2 or 3 times.

2 Preheat the oven to 100°C (210°F), or your lowest Gas Mark setting. Place the foie gras lobes in a terrine dish, packing them down well so that no air pockets remain.

3 Lift the terrine into a high-sided ovenproof dish. Pour in enough boiling water to come halfway up the sides of the terrine. Cook in the oven for 40 minutes.

4 Remove the terrine from the oven and leave it to cool. Place a board on top of it with a 250g (9oz) weight on top of that and put in the refrigerator.

5 Remove the weight and the board when the fat on top of the foie gras has set. Carefully lift the fat off and melt it in a saucepan, then drizzle it back over the top of the terrine and leave to set. Unmould the terrine and cut it into slices.

Tips

You can replace the *quatre-épices* with freshly grated nutmeg or another spice of your choice and the white port with a spirit, such as Cognac or Armagnac, or use a sweet wine if you wish.

To slice the foie gras, remove it from the refrigerator at least 20 minutes before serving. Use a lyre (a special foie gras cutter) or a thin-bladed knife to cut perfect slices. This terrine can be kept in the refrigerator for 2 weeks.

Landes Salad

SALADE LANDAISE

Serves 4

Preparation time: 20 mins

Cooking time: 3 mins

Ingredients

200g (7oz) smoked duck gizzards

2 tablespoons sherry vinegar

60g (2¼oz) walnut halves

mesclun (or other salad leaves) for 4 people

4 slices of duck foie gras (see recipe page 160), weighing about 60g (2¼oz) each

20 slices of smoked duck breast

For the vinaigrette

1 tablespoon wine vinegar of choice

1 teaspoon mustard of choice

3 tablespoons walnut oil

salt and freshly ground black pepper

This popular salad comes from the Landes area on south-west France's Atlantic coast. The region is famous for its ducks and walnuts, and these are the main ingredients in the salad. As well as smoked duck breast, it also includes gizzards and slices of foie gras.

1 Heat the gizzards in a saucepan to melt the fat. Drain the gizzards, cut them into pieces and then fry them in the pan over a high heat for 3 minutes until they are lightly golden. Pour in the vinegar, stirring with a spoon to release the cooking juices stuck to the bottom of the pan. Remove from the heat and add the walnut halves.

2 Prepare the vinaigrette. Mix the vinegar with the mustard until evenly combined, then season with salt and pepper and whisk in the oil. Toss the mesclun (or other salad leaves) with the vinaigrette.

3 Cut the slices of foie gras into pieces. Divide the mesclun (or other salad leaves) between 4 serving plates and arrange the slices of smoked duck breast, the foie gras, gizzards and walnut halves on top. Serve immediately.

Tip

You can also add dried fruits such as figs or apricots, cut into small pieces, to the salad.

Eggs Piperade

OEUFS À LA PIPERADE

Serves 6

Preparation time: 15 mins

Cooking time: 1 hour 20 mins

Ingredients

24 sweet green Basque peppers (or 6 green peppers)

1.5kg (3lb 5oz) very ripe tomatoes

3 tablespoons olive oil

3 large onions, sliced

2 garlic cloves, chopped

6 eggs

salt and freshly ground black pepper

A dish from the French Basque country made by cooking eggs with tomatoes, onions and *Doux des Landes*, a sweet green pepper that is a staple of the local cuisine and used in many recipes. The red, white and green ingredients are said to represent the Basque flag. Piperade can be served on its own as a light lunch or supper dish or as an accompaniment to meat or fish for something more substantial (see Tip).

1. Remove the stalks and seeds from the Basque peppers (as well as cores, if using regular green peppers) and cut them into strips. Plunge the tomatoes into a large saucepan of boiling water for 1 minute. Drain and cool them in a bowl of cold water, then drain again, peel off the skins and crush them.

2. Heat the oil in a large, shallow flameproof pan and sauté the onions over a low heat for about 5 minutes until softened. Add the pepper strips and the garlic and cook for another 2 minutes. Add the tomato flesh and mix well. Season with salt and pepper. Increase the heat under the pan to high so as to evaporate the liquid from the tomatoes. Lower the heat, cover the pan and leave to simmer for 1 hour, stirring from time to time.

3. Beat the eggs and pour them into the pan, stirring continuously until they are set. Serve immediately.

Tip

You can serve this dish with slices of Bayonne ham fried in 2 tablespoons of olive oil.

Duck Breasts with Caramelized Peaches

MAGRETS DE CANARD AUX PÊCHES FONDANTES

Serves 4 | **Preparation time: 20 mins** | **Cooking time: 20 mins** | **Resting time: 5 mins**

Ingredients

2 duck breasts
8 fresh peaches
30g (1oz) butter
juice of 1 orange
juice of ½ lemon
25g (1oz) sugar
salt and freshly ground black pepper

Magrets are the breasts of Mulard ducks, the most common breed of duck on French farms, that have been raised for foie gras. In this recipe, the duck breasts are served with fresh peaches cooked in butter and citrus juices before being sprinkled with sugar to caramelize them. When fresh local peaches are not available, other fruits, either fresh or canned, can be caramelized in the same way.

1 Cut several slashes diagonally in the skin of the duck breasts using a sharp knife.

2 Bring a saucepan of water to the boil. Immerse the peaches in the water for 3 minutes to blanch them. Drain the peaches, cool them under cold running water and then peel off their skins. Cut the peaches in half, remove the stones and set aside.

3 Melt the butter in a frying pan. Add the orange and lemon juices and the peach halves and dust them with the sugar. Cook for 15 minutes over a gentle heat, letting the fruits caramelize, adding a tablespoon of water if necessary.

4 Meanwhile, fry the duck breasts in another pan without adding any fat over a medium heat, skin side down to begin with, for about 5 minutes. Pour off the fat rendered by the duck breasts and cook for another 5 minutes on each side. Season with salt and pepper.

5 Leave the duck breasts to rest for about 5 minutes, covered in foil to keep them warm, then serve immediately with the roasted caramelized peaches.

Duck Confit with Sarladaise Potatoes

CONFIT SARLADAIS

Serves 6 | **Preparation time: 30 mins** | **Chilling time: 12 hours** | **Cooking time: 3½ hours**

Ingredients

100g (3½oz) coarse salt
6 fattened duck legs
500g (1lb 2oz) duck fat
500g (1lb 2oz) firm-fleshed potatoes
3 garlic cloves, crushed
1 bunch of parsley, chopped
salt and freshly ground black pepper

Pommes de terre sarladaises **are potatoes that have been fried in duck or goose fat with garlic and parsley and they are traditionally served with duck confit. They take their name from the small medieval town of Sarlat-la-Canéda in the Dordogne, which is famous for its foie gras. Duck confit, originally a speciality of Gascony, is a centuries-old way of preserving duck legs in their own fat so that they could be kept for long periods before the invention of refrigerators and freezers. The duck legs are first rubbed with salt and then slowly cooked until very tender. The cooked legs are then transferred to a jar or other container and their fat poured over, covering the legs completely.**

1 The day before, rub the coarse salt over the duck legs and leave them in the refrigerator overnight or for at least 12 hours.

2 The next day, remove the salt from the duck legs, rinse them thoroughly and pat them dry with kitchen paper. Melt the duck fat in a flameproof casserole or large, heavy-based saucepan over a very gentle heat.

3 Place the duck legs in the hot fat and leave them to cook for 3 hours over a very low heat, making sure that the meat does not stick to the bottom of the pan. The cooking temperature of the duck fat must not go higher than 80°C (176°F).

4 If using new potatoes, wash them well and pat them dry with kitchen paper. Otherwise, halve or quarter the potatoes or leave them whole, depending on their size.

5 Remove 50g (1¾oz) of the duck fat used to cook the legs. Add this to a hot frying pan and fry the potatoes for 30 minutes, turning them over frequently. Season with salt and pepper.

6 Meanwhile, drain the duck legs from the remaining fat and cook them for 5 minutes on each side in a hot nonstick frying pan over a medium heat.

7 Sprinkle the potatoes with the crushed garlic and chopped parsley, mixing them gently with the potatoes. Serve immediately with the confit duck legs.

Tip

The confit duck legs can be stored covered in their fat for 2–3 weeks in the refrigerator.

Béarnaise Chicken in a Pot

POULE AU POT BÉARNAISE

Serves 8

Preparation time: 30 mins

Cooking time: 1½–2 hours

Ingredients

1 chicken, weighing about 3kg (6lb 8oz), with its liver, heart and gizzard

200g (7oz) stale sandwich bread, plus several extra slices for toasting

2 onions, 1 chopped and 1 left whole

1 garlic clove, chopped

200g (7oz) Bayonne ham, chopped

½ bunch of flat leaf parsley, chopped

2 eggs, beaten

2 cloves

4 leeks, trimmed, cleaned and cut into short lengths

8 carrots, cut into large pieces

4 turnips, quartered

1 small swede, quartered (optional)

1 head of curly kale, chopped

1 celery stick, chopped

a few whole black peppercorns

1 bouquet garni

salt and freshly ground black pepper

This recipe for a whole chicken stuffed with ham, onions, garlic, parsley and offal before being slowly poached in water is from the Béarn region in the Pyrenee. It owes its fame to Henri IV of France, who came from the town of Pau. In the 17th century, the king declared it France's national dish. In an attempt to combat the famine caused by the lengthy religious wars between Huguenots and Catholics, he declared that, in return for God sparing his life: 'I will ensure every working man in my kingdom will have a chicken to cook for their Sunday dinner.'

1 Prepare the stuffing. Chop up the chicken liver, heart and gizzard. Blitz the 200g (7oz) of bread to breadcrumbs in a food processor. Mix together the chopped onion, garlic, ham, parsley and chicken liver, heart and gizzard in a large mixing bowl, then add the breadcrumbs and beaten eggs and season with salt and pepper, stirring until all the ingredients are well combined. Spoon the stuffing into the cavity of the chicken and, using thin kitchen string, carefully sew the opening together.

2 Put the chicken in a large saucepan and cover it with cold water. Bring the water to the boil, skimming the surface several times to remove the foam. Season with salt, then half-cover the pan, lower the heat and cook for 30 minutes with the water just simmering gently.

3 Stick the cloves into the whole peeled onion. Add all the vegetables to the pan with the peppercorns and bouquet garni.

4 Continue to cook the chicken for another 1–1½ hours until the flesh is tender.

5 Toast the slices of bread and place them at the bottom of a soup tureen.

6 Lift the chicken out of the pan and place it in a serving dish. Drain the vegetables with a slotted spoon and put them in a separate dish or around the chicken. Pour the cooking liquid over the slices of toast in the soup tureen. Take the chicken to the table, carve or divide it into joints and remove the stuffing. Cut the stuffing into slices and serve hot with the chicken, with the soup-soaked bread alongside.

Tip

Serve the chicken on its own or accompanied with gherkins or *sauce gribiche*, a classic French sauce made with chopped hard-boiled eggs, mustard, olive oil, fresh herbs, capers and gherkins.

SABATIER

Cep and Ham Casserole

DAUBE DE CÈPES

Serves 6–8

Preparation time: 30 mins

Cooking time: 1 hour 50 mins

Ingredients

2kg (4lb 8oz) firm fresh ceps

3 tablespoons goose fat (or duck fat or oil)

10 garlic cloves, chopped

3 shallots, chopped

2 slices of ham, chopped

2 slices of lean pork belly, streaky bacon or pancetta, chopped

250ml (9fl oz) water or vegetable or chicken stock

200ml (7fl oz) dry white wine

1 parsley sprig, chopped

Cep is one of the most highly prized mushrooms and it is easy to recognize due to its sturdy stem and rounded brown cap that resembles a crusty brown roll, hence its nickname 'penny bun'. In season from the beginning of August to the end of October, ceps can be foraged in woodland areas, especially those with beech, oak or pine trees. In south-west France, *ventrèche maigre* would be used for this dish – pork belly that is cured by salting and then seasoning with pepper before being left to dry.

1 Clean the ceps thoroughly with a clean cloth or kitchen paper, without washing them. Cut them in half lengthways.

2 Heat half the goose fat (or duck fat or oil) in a large frying pan and fry the ceps until golden. Drain them from the pan and set aside. Add the garlic, shallots, ham and pork belly, bacon or pancetta to the pan and fry over a low heat for 20 minutes.

3 Return the ceps to the pan, cover and simmer for 20 minutes.

4 Transfer the contents of the pan to a flameproof casserole and pour in the water or stock and wine. Cover the casserole and leave to simmer over a very low heat for 1 hour – the longer the casserole is simmered for, the better it will be. Serve with the chopped parsley sprinkled over.

Tip

This dish can be served as an accompaniment to a duck confit (see recipe page 168) or grilled steak, or eaten on its own.

Garbure

Serves 8

Preparation time: 40 mins

Soaking time: 12 hours

Cooking time: 2½ hours

Ingredients

1 Bayonne ham heel (or joint), boned

300g (10½oz) dried white haricot beans

200g (7oz) shelled fresh broad beans (or frozen, defrosted)

2 Toulouse sausages

3 confit duck legs (page 168)

1 bouquet garni

2 litres (3½ pints) chicken stock (or water)

200ml (7fl oz) dry white wine

2 shallots, finely sliced

2 carrots, cut into small pieces

2 turnips, cut into small pieces

white parts of 2 leeks, trimmed, cleaned and finely chopped

1 celery stick, finely chopped

¼ green cabbage, leaves cut into strips

500g (1lb 2oz) potatoes, cut into small pieces

6–8 slices of country bread

3 garlic cloves, peeled

1 tablespoon chopped parsley

salt and freshly ground black pepper

***Garbure* is a thick soup from Gascony, the word deriving from *'garb'*, which describes grain when it is shown on a coat of arms or shield. A *garbure* was a pitchfork that was once used to harvest the sheaves of grain, and as the dish is eaten with a fork, its name is a reference to that.**

1 The day before, soak the ham and the dried haricot beans in separate bowls of cold water overnight or for 12 hours.

2 The next day, drain the ham and blanch it in a saucepan of boiling water for 10 minutes, then drain. Peel the skins off the broad beans.

3 Preheat the oven to 220°C (425°F), Gas Mark 7. Put the Toulouse sausages and confit duck legs (reserving the fat) in a roasting tin and roast them for 15 minutes until golden. Drain from the fat and cut the sausages and duck leg meat into large pieces. Set aside.

4 Put the ham, soaked haricot beans and bouquet garni in a large flameproof casserole. Pour in the stock (or water) and bring to the boil, then lower the heat and simmer for 45 minutes. Deglaze the roasting tin with the wine, then add the juices to the casserole.

5 Heat a little of the reserved duck fat in a sauté pan and fry the shallots, carrots, turnips, leeks and celery for 5 minutes. Season with salt and pepper, then add the vegetables to the casserole and simmer for 30 minutes.

6 Blanch the cabbage for 5–8 minutes in a saucepan of salted boiling water, without covering the pan. Drain and add it to the casserole with the potatoes. Simmer for another 30 minutes. Add the broad beans and cook them for 5 minutes. Adjust the seasoning, adding more salt and pepper as needed, and remove the bouquet garni.

7 Toast the slices of bread and rub them with the garlic cloves. Cut the ham into 1cm (½-inch) slices and return to the casserole, adding the sausages and duck leg meat as well. Sprinkle over the parsley and bring back to the boil, adding a few extra grinds of pepper if necessary. Serve immediately with the toasted slices of garlic bread.

Toulouse Cassoulet

CASSOULET DE TOULOUSE

Serves 6

Preparation time: 40 mins

Soaking time: 6–12 hours

Cooking time: 2½ hours

Ingredients

800g (1lb 12oz) dried white kidney beans (*lingots*)

250g (9oz) pork skin

150g (5½oz) goose fat

500g (1lb 2oz) boneless shoulder (or neck) of mutton or lamb (optional), cut into pieces

3 onions, 2 sliced into rounds, 1 chopped

11 garlic cloves, peeled

250ml (9fl oz) chicken stock

300g (10½oz) boneless pork loin (or shoulder cut from the blade bone), cut into large cubes

150g (5½oz) cured French country ham, diced

2 carrots, peeled and chopped

250g (9oz) pork spare ribs

1 bouquet garni

a little freshly grated nutmeg

400g (14oz) goose or duck confit (see page 168)

250g (9oz) Toulouse sausages

salt and freshly ground black pepper

Many places in south-west France lay claim to having made the first cassoulet, but it is generally agreed that the honour should go to Castelnaudary. Legend has it that in this small town, 55 kilometres (34 miles) from Toulouse, when the residents were facing starvation during the Hundred Years War with the English they threw beans, sausages, duck and any other scraps they had into a giant cooking pot called a *cassole*, and the first cassoulet was born.

1 Soak the beans in a bowl of cold water for a minimum of 6 hours and up to 12 hours, changing the water several times. In a separate bowl, soak the pork skin in cold water.

2 Heat 50g (1¾oz) of the goose fat in a large flameproof casserole over a medium heat and fry the mutton or lamb pieces (if using) until browned all over. Add the sliced onions and 4 garlic cloves. Season with salt and pepper and pour in the stock. Cover the casserole and leave it to simmer for 40 minutes.

3 Meanwhile, drain the pork skin and cut it into small strips. Boil it in a saucepan of water for 10 minutes, then drain.

4 Heat another 50g (1¾oz) of goose fat in a separate flameproof casserole over a medium heat and fry the pork meat, ham, carrots, chopped onion and spare ribs for 10 minutes until lightly browned. Season with salt and pepper. Drain the soaked beans and add with the pork skin, remaining 7 garlic cloves, the bouquet garni and nutmeg. Pour enough boiling into the casserole to cover the beans by about 3cm (1¼ inches). Cover the casserole and leave the cassoulet to simmer very gently, regularly skimming any foam from the surface, for 45–50 minutes.

5 Add the mutton or lamb (if using) and onion mixture and gently mix in. Scrape the fat off the confit goose (or duck) and add the meat to the casserole. Cover and cook for another 30 minutes.

6 Prick the sausages all over with a fork. Heat the remaining goose fat in a frying pan over a medium heat and fry the sausages until well browned on all sides. Drain them from the pan.

7 Add the sausages to the casserole, cutting them into 6 to ensure each portion contains a piece, and serve the cassoulet piping hot.

LONG LIVE
PORK CHARCUTERIE!

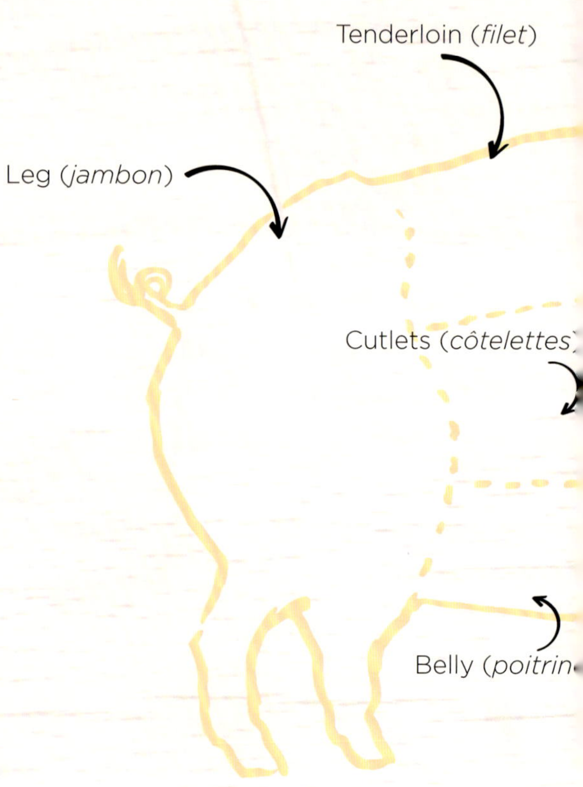

Normandy's Andouille de Vire or Brittany's Andouille de Guémené: the Choice is Yours

This type of sausage measures 25–30cm (10–12 inches) and is made from the intestines and parts of a pig's stomach that are cut up and enclosed in a natural casing. The ingredients in an andouille tend to give it a rather negative reputation, but you do not need a strong stomach to relish this tasty speciality. Long cold-smoking over beech wood gives the sausage its characteristic black colour. It is then tied with string, cooked in a court bouillon (stock) and eaten cold, cut into thin slices.

Dry-cured Sausage, a Star of the Auvergne

Sausages are not the only speciality of the Auvergne, but if we had to pick one outstanding product of the region, it would be its dry-cured sausage, *saucisson sec* (which is unquestionably good, but then so are its lentils). The sausage is renowned for its unique flavour and aroma, due to the special blend of herbs and spices it contains. The ingredients that most commonly flavour it are black pepper, red wine, garlic and thyme. The pigs from which the *saucisson* is made must be fed on local cereals, and the meat used has to be pure pork with a fat content lower than that of standard sausage recipes. Compliance with these manufacturing regulations, as well as the length of time it takes to make it, earned this dry Auvergne sausage, eaten cold and sliced – plus the Auvergne's other dry sausage, *saucisse sèche* – European IGP certification in 2016.

The Battle of the Rillettes

The origins of rillettes are claimed by two towns, Le Mans and Tours. The two rillettes look the same, but the way they are made differs a little. Both are produced from pork, but the rillettes from Le Mans are simmered slowly and mixed with the fat produced, while the rillettes from Tours are cooked quickly, often with the pig's liver added. What they do have in common is that they have no flavourings other than a seasoning of salt and pepper. If one of them must claim first place on the podium, it would perhaps be the Touraine rillettes due to its IGP classification, as it gives it official recognition of the history of rillettes-making in this region.

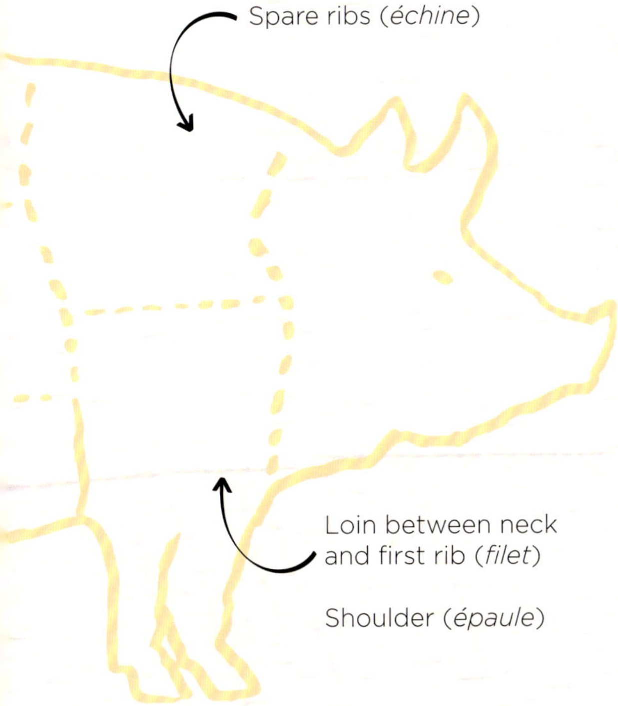

The Charcuterie-lover's Paradise

Pork enthusiasts are bound to be delighted when visiting the city of Lyon, which has made charcuterie and tripe specialities the flagship of its traditional cuisine. There are the classic Lyon sausages, with finely chopped lean meat and coarsely chopped fat, the brioche sausage, often studded with pistachios, and the incomparable *rosette*, which is delicious eaten with gherkins. But there are other more typical specialities that make the city famous, even more so than its region, such as veal andouillette, *pâté de tête* (brawn made with pig's head and tongue), *gras-double* (tripe sautéed and seasoned with vinegar) or *le tablier de sapeur* (breaded grilled tripe). In Lyon's *bouchons* (traditional restaurants famous for their home-cooked local dishes made with fresh ingredients and their friendly atmosphere), the most adventurous gourmets might also be tempted by *pieds de mouton* (sheep's trotters), *paquets de couennes* (small pork skin parcels that are slowly simmered in stock with carrots, onions and parsley) or even *museau de boeuf en salade* (ox snout dressed with vinaigrette, capers, fresh herbs and onion).

Spare ribs (*échine*)

Loin between neck and first rib (*filet*)

Shoulder (*épaule*)

Not Forgetting the Black Pudding

And not just any black pudding either, but the Caribbean black pudding (blood sausage), a variation on the traditional black pudding. It is still made with pork fat and blood, but also features a mixture of spices and aromatics such as chive sprigs, *quatre-épices* (see page 160) chilli or even a clove that give it a unique flavour and make it spicier than its French cousin. It is usually poached, then sliced and grilled.

Figatellu, Prisuttu and Lonzo

Corsican charcuterie is one of the most famous and delicious in France. It is made mainly from pork and results from centuries of know-how passed down from generation to generation throughout the island. Raised outdoors, the pigs have a natural diet, which gives the charcuterie an exceptional quality and taste. The most famous of the island's specialities are *lonzu*, *coppa*, Italian *figatellu*, *prisuttu* and Corsican sausage, which are usually offered as an accompaniment to an aperitif or even, in the case of *figatellu*, sautéed and served as a main course. In recognition of its excellence, Corsican charcuterie regularly wins awards at fine food competitions.

Piquillo Peppers Stuffed with Salt Cod

PIMENTS 'PIQUILLOS' FARCIS À LA MORUE

Serves 6

Preparation time: 45 mins

Soaking time: 24 hours

Cooking time: 20–30 mins

Ingredients

1kg (2lb 4oz) dried salt cod

24 *piquillo* chilli peppers (or 6 red peppers)

2 large onions, chopped

2 tablespoons olive oil

1 garlic clove, crushed

pinch of Piment d'Espelette

200ml (7fl oz) tomato pasta sauce

salt

In the Basque Country, this dish would be made with *piquillos*, small red, heart-shaped chilli peppers. Fresh ones are difficult to find outside of south-west France, but they can be bought preserved in jars and cans from major supermarkets and delicatessens. Simply drain the peppers and pat them dry with kitchen paper before stuffing. Piment d'Espelette is a spice made from a variety of chilli that grows in the Basque region of France and is named after the village of Espelette. It adds a subtle rather than fiery heat to dishes.

1 The day before, cut the salt cod into large pieces and soak them in a bowl of cold water for 24 hours to remove the excess salt, changing the water several times.

2 The next day, drain the salt cod pieces and put them in a flameproof casserole. Cover them completely with cold water and begin cooking them over a high heat, but as soon as the water starts to tremble, turn off the heat and cover the casserole. Leave the salt cod in its cooking liquid for another 5 minutes.

3 Drain the salt cod, remove the skin and bones, and flake the flesh.

4 Cut the stalks off the *piquillos* and remove the seeds. If you are using regular red peppers, place them whole under a hot oven grill and grill on all sides until their skins are blistered. Remove from the grill and wrap them in damp kitchen paper. Leave to cool, then peel off the skins and remove the stalks, cores and seeds.

5 Gently fry the onions in the oil in a sauté pan. Add the flaked salt cod, garlic and Piment d'Espelette. Cover the pan and leave to cook over a low heat for 15 minutes. Transfer the mixture to a shallow dish and, using a fork, crush roughly to form a coarse purée. Season (very lightly) with salt, if necessary.

6 Fill the *piquillos* (or the red peppers) with the salt cod mixture. Serve immediately with the tomato sauce, either warm or cold.

Landes Pastis

PASTIS LANDAIS

Makes 2 pastis

Preparation time: 20 mins

Resting time: 6½–7 hours

Cooking time: 45 mins

Ingredients

30g (1oz) fresh yeast (or 2 × 7g/¼oz sachets fast-action dried yeast)

3–4 tablespoons warm milk, plus extra to glaze

5 eggs

200g (7oz) icing sugar

pinch of salt

3 tablespoons rum

175g (6oz) butter, softened, plus extra for greasing

500g–750g (1lb 2oz–1lb 10oz) plain flour

50g (1¾oz) pearl/nib sugar

There are two kinds of pastis in Gascony: the Landes pastis, which is this cake made with a yeast dough, and the Armagnac pastis (or Gascony pastis), a type of puff pastry crown called a *croustade* or *tourtière* in the Landes.

1 If using fresh yeast, dissolve it in the warm milk.

2 Break the eggs into a mixing bowl and lightly beat them. Add the icing sugar, salt, rum and butter. Whisk until evenly mixed then add the dissolved fresh yeast (if using) and milk. Mix again and gradually add enough flour (with the dried yeast, if using), working the dough with your hands until it is smooth and does not stick to your fingers.

3 Knead the dough for 2–3 minutes. Shape it into a ball, then put it into a clean bowl, cover with a clean tea towel and leave it to rise at room temperature for 6 hours, punching it down and briefly kneading it again every 2 hours.

4 Grease two 20cm (8-inch) brioche tins with butter. Divide the dough in half and place in the tins. Cover with the tea towel and leave the dough to rise again for 30 minutes–1 hour until it reaches the top of the tins. Meanwhile, preheat the oven to 180°C (350°F), Gas Mark 4. Brush the tops of the dough with milk and sprinkle with the pearl/nib sugar.

5 Bake for 45 minutes. Remove from the oven and leave to cool for a few minutes in the tins, then turn out on to a wire rack to cool further. Eat warm or cold.

Pumpkin 'Milhassou'

MILHASSOU AU POTIRON

Serves 8

Preparation time: 20 mins

Cooking time: 1½ hours

Ingredients

500g (1lb 2oz) pumpkin, peeled weight

200g (7oz) cornflour

150g (5½oz) sugar

80g (3oz) butter, softened, plus extra for greasing

5 eggs

pinch of salt

500ml (18fl oz) milk

50ml (2fl oz) rum

a few drops vanilla extract

There are many different ways of making this pumpkin pie, known as a *milhassou* (or *millasou*). It can be sweet or less sweet, with added flavourings such as Armagnac, orange flower water and rum, among others. Sometimes the pie is baked with prunes, and traditionally millet was also used to make it, from which its name is derived.

1 Remove the fibrous strands and the seeds from the pumpkin flesh and cut it into pieces. Put 200ml (7fl oz) water in a saucepan and add the pumpkin pieces, then cover the pan and cook over a low heat for about 30 minutes until the pumpkin flesh is very soft. Drain it, then pass it through a vegetable mill or blend in a blender to a smooth purée.

2 Transfer the pumpkin purée to a mixing bowl, add the cornflour and stir until evenly combined. Then beat in the sugar, butter, the eggs, one at a time and mixing well after each egg is added, and the salt. Gradually beat in the milk, followed by the rum and vanilla extract.

3 Preheat the oven to 200°C (400°F), Gas Mark 6. Grease a 24cm (9½-inch) flan tin with butter, pour the pumpkin mixture into it and bake for 1 hour. Carefully turn the *milhassou* out and serve it warm or cold.

Basque Cake

GÂTEAU BASQUE

Serves 6–8

Preparation time: 30 mins

Resting time: 1 hour

Cooking time: 40 mins

Ingredients

300g (10½oz) plain flour

150g (5½oz) sugar

pinch of salt

1½ teaspoons baking powder

1 egg, plus 3 egg yolks

150g (5½oz) butter, cut into small pieces and softened, plus extra for greasing

1–2 tablespoons rum

400g (14oz) black Itxassou cherry jam (see page 222) or artisan cherry preserve

1 tablespoon milk

icing sugar, for dusting (optional)

This cake can also be made with a custard filling instead of the black cherry jam used here. It is decorated by placing a stencil on top with the cut-out shape of the *lauburu*, an ancient hooked cross with four comma-shaped heads that is the traditional symbol of the Basque Country and its people, dusting icing sugar over it before carefully lifting off the stencil.

1 First make the dough. Mix together the flour, sugar, salt and baking powder in a mixing bowl. Make a well in the centre and add the whole egg and 2 egg yolks, the butter and rum. Using a wooden spoon, mix the ingredients together, starting at the centre and working outwards, then knead the dough with your hands until it is smooth. Shape it into a ball, wrap it in greaseproof paper and leave to rest for 1 hour in the refrigerator.

2 Divide the dough into 2 pieces, one two-thirds and the other one-third. Generously grease a 26cm (10½-inch) cake tin with butter. Roll out the larger piece of dough and use to line the base and sides of the tin.

3 Preheat the oven to 200°C (400°F), Gas Mark 6. Spread the jam over the pastry base. Roll out the smaller piece of dough to make a lid. Dampen the edges of the pastry case, place the lid on top and press the edges together to seal. Beat the remaining egg yolk with the milk and brush over the lid to glaze.

4 Bake for 20 minutes, then lower the temperature to 180°C (350°F), Gas Mark 4, and bake for another 20 minutes. Remove the cake from the oven and leave it to cool in the tin until it is still warm but no longer hot before unmoulding it. Serve warm or cold, decorated with the Basque cross dusted in icing sugar on top, if you wish.

Tarn Shuttles

NAVETTES TARNAISES

Makes 1kg (2lb 4oz) biscuits

Preparation time: 30 mins

Cooking time: 10–15 mins

Ingredients

200g (7oz) whole blanched almonds

230g (8oz) sugar

400g (14oz) plain flour

200g (7oz) butter, softened

2 eggs

50ml (2fl oz) rum

These small biscuits take their name from the diamond-shaped shuttle that carried the thread of the weft yarn when weaving with a loom. There were many weavers in south-west France during the time of the Cathars and these biscuits are a speciality of several towns in Occitanie, from Castelnaudary as far as Marseille.

1 Using a pestle and mortar (or in a bowl and using the end of a rolling pin), crush the almonds with 50g (1¾oz) of the sugar.

2 Sift the flour into a mixing bowl. Make a well in the centre and add 150g (5½oz) of the sugar, followed by the butter, eggs, rum and crushed almonds, mixing thoroughly each time you add a new ingredient. Work the dough with your hands until it is smooth.

3 Preheat the oven to 180°C (350°F), Gas Mark 4. Line a baking sheet lined with nonstick baker paper. Using your hands, roll the dough into small balls, then shape them into boat shapes. Place them on the lined baking sheet and mark a line lengthways down the centre of each one with the back of a knife. Dust the tops of the biscuits with the remaining sugar and bake them for 10–15 minutes until they are golden brown.

The Massif Central

AND LYONNAIS

Cousina or Chestnut Soup

COUSINA OU SOUPE DE CHÂTAIGNES

Serves 6

Preparation time: 40 mins if using fresh chestnuts; 15 mins if using canned/vacuum-packed

Cooking time: 1 hour 5 mins if using fresh chestnuts; 35 mins if using canned/vacuum-packed

Ingredients

1kg (2lb 4oz) fresh chestnuts (or canned or vacuum-packed)

7 or 8 celery sticks, chopped

1.5 litres (2¾ pints) chicken stock

freshly grated nutmeg

500ml (18fl oz) crème fraîche

salt and freshly ground black pepper

In France, people often gather their own chestnuts rather than buying them, and there are two distinct types: *marron* and *châtaigne*. *Châtaignes* have twin nuts inside the same shell, whereas *marrons* have just one and are the type used to make *marrons glacés*. Cousina is made using the *châtaigne* chestnuts that grow in the Ardèche region and have their own AOC certification.

1 If you are using fresh chestnuts, you will need to peel and cook them. Cut a small incision in the shell of each chestnut with a small sharp knife, taking care not to pierce the skin underneath it.

2 Plunge the chestnuts into a saucepan of boiling water for 5 minutes. Gradually remove them from the pan, peeling off the shells while they are still hot. The two coverings, the shell and the skin, should then peel off easily. Return the peeled chestnuts to the pan and cover with cold water. Bring to the boil and leave to cook for 25 minutes, then drain.

3 Set aside about 10 of the chestnuts. Blend the rest to a purée in a food processor or pass through a vegetable mill. Put the purée in a large saucepan with the celery and pour in the stock. Stir to mix well and then simmer for 30 minutes. Season with salt and pepper and add a little grated nutmeg.

4 At the end of the cooking time, the soup should be thick. Whisk in the crème fraîche and adjust the seasoning. Bring to the boil, then add most of the reserved whole chestnuts. Chop the rest finely. Cook for another 1–2 minutes then pour the soup into tureens and serve immediately, garnished with the chopped chestnuts.

Potato Pie

PÂTÉ AUX POMMES DE TERRE

Serves 6–8

Preparation time: 40 mins

Resting time: 2 hours

Cooking time: 55 mins

Ingredients

For the pastry

300g (10½oz) plain flour, plus extra for dusting

150g (5½oz) butter, cut into small pieces and softened

pinch of salt

1 egg

For the filling

800g (1lb 12oz) firm-fleshed potatoes

1 litre (1¾ pints) milk, plus 2 tablespoons to glaze

1 tablespoon butter, plus extra for greasing

1 tablespoon oil

150g (5½oz) smoked bacon lardons

2 onions, sliced

2 tablespoons mixed chopped chives and parsley

1 egg yolk

200ml (7fl oz) liquid crème fraîche

salt and freshly ground black pepper

This pie is a speciality of central France, and as well as sliced potatoes, the filling contains crème fraîche, smoked bacon, onions and fresh herbs. Eaten hot, the pie can be served on its own or accompanied with a green salad.

1 First make the pastry. Sift the flour into a mixing bowl. Make a well in the centre and add the butter, salt, egg and 200ml (7fl oz) cold water. Work the ingredients together with your fingertips to make a firm dough. Shape it into a ball, cover with greaseproof paper and leave to rest in a cool place for 2 hours.

2 Meanwhile prepare the filling. Peel the potatoes and slice them into thin rounds. Bring the milk to the boil in a large saucepan. Remove it from the heat, add the sliced potatoes and leave them in the milk for about 30 minutes.

3 Heat the butter and oil in a frying pan and fry the bacon lardons until golden brown. Remove and set aside in a large bowl. Add the onions to the pan and fry until softened but not coloured. Add to the bacon with the chives and parsley. Drain the potato slices and add those as well. Season with a little salt and pepper and mix everything together.

4 Preheat the oven to 200°C (400°F), Gas Mark 6. Divide the pastry dough into 2 pieces, one two-thirds and the other one-third. Roll out both pieces on a lightly floured work surface into circles 2mm (1/16 inch) thick. Grease a 25cm (10-inch) pie dish and line it with the larger circle of pastry, leaving a border of 3cm (1¼ inches) overhanging the edge. Spoon in the potato, bacon and onion mixture. Fold down the excess pastry around the edge and brush with cold water. Lay the smaller circle of pastry on top and trim to fit the pie as necessary. Press the pastry edges gently together to seal them. Beat the egg yolk with the 2 tablespoons of milk and brush it over the pastry to glaze. Cut a small hole in the centre of the pastry lid and push a small, rolled-up piece of cardboard into it to make a chimney.

5 Bake the pie for 45 minutes. Towards the end of the cooking time, check that the pastry is sufficiently browned and lower the oven temperature to 170–180°C (340–350°F), Gas Mark 3½–4, if necessary. When the pie is cooked, slowly pour the liquid crème fraîche down the chimney into the filling. Serve immediately.

Canut's Brain

CERVELLE DE CANUT

Serves 4

Preparation time: 10 mins

Draining time: 12 hours

Ingredients

400g (14oz) fromage blanc (or use ricotta or a soft goats' cheese)

2 tablespoons crème fraîche

100g (3½oz) chopped fresh mixed herbs, such as chives, chervil and parsley, plus extra to garnish

1 garlic clove, chopped

1 shallot, chopped

2 tablespoons dry white wine

2 tablespoons sherry vinegar

salt and freshly ground black pepper

This recipe, made by stirring fresh herbs, garlic and shallots into soft fresh cheese, can be served spread on toasted bread and savoury biscuits or as a party dip with vegetable crudités. Much enjoyed by the inhabitants of Lyon today, just as the *canuts*, the silk workers of 19th-century Lyon, did before them.

1. The day before, put the cheese in a sieve lined with muslin placed over a bowl. Leave to drain overnight or for 12 hours in the refrigerator.
2. The next day, whisk together the drained cheese, crème fraîche and salt and pepper in a mixing bowl. Stir in the chopped herbs, garlic and shallot. Add the wine and vinegar and stir again until evenly mixed.
3. Keep in the refrigerator in a bowl covered with clingfilm until ready to serve. Garnish with extra fresh herbs sprinkled over and accompany with, for example, toasted bread.

SOME DISHES YOU MIGHT NOT KNOW

BUT THEY ARE VERY TASTY!

BOUILLABAISSE

Marseille, nicknamed the Phocaean city after the Greek sailors from Phocaea in Asia Minor who founded it in 600 BC, is famous for its not-to-be missed speciality, bouillabaisse. This hearty fish soup takes its name from two Provençal words *bouia* (to boil) and *baisso* (to reduce), and to protect the classic recipe from the many wildly diverse copies that were circulating, a *Charte de la bouillabaisse* was established by a group of Marseille restaurateurs in 1980.

See recipe page 294.

Cervelle De Canut

In English it means 'Canut's brain', but don't shudder at the thought, as it is not what you might think! It is, in fact, a delicious fresh cheese spread. Until the end of the 19th century, cheese was considered the meat of the poor because it was rich in protein but much less expensive than sheep's brains, and the silk workers of the Lyonnais region, who were known as *canuts*, therefore ate it regularly.

See recipe page 196.

CLAQUEBITOU

Originating in Burgundy, this fresh goats' cheese, which is bathed in its own whey, has the even stranger name in Burgundian dialect of *quiaque-bitou*. According to popular etymology, the local word *bitou* is associated with the eye and this speciality would indeed have once been used as a remedy for eye diseases!

See recipe page 126.

Échaudés

Translating literally as 'scalded', these traditional pastries from the Aveyron region live up to their name, as the first step when making the dough is to poach it in hot water before baking it in the oven.

See recipe page 226.

MILHASSOU

This is certainly a very fancy way of describing a pumpkin dessert! The name comes from the millet that was – and sometimes still is – traditionally used to make it.

See recipe page 184.

FLAMMENKÜCHE

If you have trouble pronouncing the name of this in a restaurant, don't give up just yet, as it is the Flemish word for a delicious flambéed tart.

See recipe page 232.

Oreillettes

Oreillettes might mean 'headsets/earpieces' in English, but these are definitely not the latest fashionable earbuds, rather a type of fritter from the Languedoc. The history behind their name is unclear, although some say it comes from the traditional ear-like shape of these little sweet indulgences.

See recipe page 302.

Kig Ha Farz

You can almost smell the sea spray in this dish from Finistère. Kig Ha Farz, which translates as 'meat and flour' in the Breton dialect, is an essential part of Brittany's culinary tradition.

See recipe page 58.

POTJEVLEESH & WATERZOÏ

By all means practise pronouncing the names of these two dishes because once you've tried them you might find you want to order them regularly! *Potjevleesh* translates from Flemish as 'meat in a small pot', while *waterzoï* is the rather less inspiring 'boiling water'.

See recipes pages 18 and 20.

Sausage in Brioche

SAUCISSON BRIOCHÉ

Serves 6

Preparation time: 15 mins

Resting time: 20 mins

Cooking time: 40 mins

Ingredients

1 Lyonnais poaching sausage (*saucisson de Lyon à cuire*)

3 eggs

250g (9oz) plain flour, plus extra for dusting

2½ teaspoons baking powder

150ml (5fl oz) crème fraîche

butter, for greasing

This is a classic recipe from the city of Lyon where a whole sausage is wrapped in brioche and then baked until golden brown. Normally made with butter, this variation on the traditional brioche dough uses crème fraîche instead to enrich it. Serve cut into slices as a starter or as a main course with a green salad.

1 Bring a saucepan of water to the boil and poach the sausage for 15 minutes, then drain.

2 Crack the eggs into a mixing bowl. Sift in the flour and baking powder and stir in the crème fraîche.

3 Using a spatula, work the ingredients together to make a smooth dough. Divide into two equal pieces.

4 Grease a 22cm (8½-inch) loaf tin with butter and dust it with flour. Press half the dough into the tin. Place the sausage in the middle and cover with the remaining dough.

5 Cover the tin with a clean tea towel and leave to rest for 20 minutes. Meanwhile, preheat the oven to 200°C (400°F), Gas Mark 6.

6 Bake the sausage in brioche for 40 minutes until golden brown. Remove from the oven and leave the brioche to cool in the tin for 15 minutes, then turn out, slice and serve warm.

Lyonnais Onion Soup

GRATINÉE LYONNAISE

Serves 4

Preparation time: 20 mins

Cooking time: 1¼ hours

Ingredients

1kg (2lb 4oz) onions, finely sliced

50g (1¾oz) butter

2 tablespoons plain flour

1 litre (1¾ pints) beef (or chicken) stock

1 bouquet garni

300g (10½oz) Emmental cheese

thin slices of bread

100ml (3½fl oz) ruby port

salt and freshly ground black pepper

This Lyonnais version of onion soup comes from Forez, a mountainous region in the Massif Central, which has made the onion its favourite vegetable, using it in a variety of different ways. Traditionally topped with a bread and cheese crust *(gratinée)*, alongside onion confit, it is served with grilled steak or as an accompaniment to *gras-double* (tripe sautéed and seasoned with vinegar).

1 Sweat the onions in the butter in a large saucepan, covered with a lid, over a gentle heat for about 20 minutes until they are softened. Then uncover and cook over a high heat until the onions are golden brown, stirring from time to time. Dust the onions with the flour, stir until they are coated and cook for 2–3 minutes, stirring continuously. Add the stock, still stirring, and then the bouquet garni. Bring to the boil, season with salt and pepper and cook over a low heat for 30 minutes.

2 Grate half the Emmental and cut the rest into thin slices. Toast the slices of bread. Layer a slice of toasted bread, a slice of Emmental, a slice of toasted bread and some of the grated Emmental in 4 individual ovenproof serving bowls, standing on a baking sheet. Finish with a slice of toasted bread.

3 Preheat the oven to 200°C (400°F), Gas Mark 6. Stir the port into the onion soup, discarding the bouquet garni, then ladle enough soup into the bowls to cover the toast. Place in the oven and cook for 10 minutes. Add the remaining soup, top with the remaining grated Emmental and return to the oven for another 5 minutes or until the cheese has melted and browned. Serve immediately while the soup is still very hot.

Ardèche Criques

CRIQUES ARDÉCHOISES

Serves 4

Preparation time: 15 mins

Cooking time: 20 mins per pancake

Ingredients

4 large potatoes

4 eggs

4 tablespoons crème fraîche

2 garlic cloves, chopped

3 tablespoons chopped parsley, plus extra to garnish

120g (4¼oz) butter

salt and freshly ground black pepper

These thick potato pancakes are one of the Ardèche region's most famous dishes. Made from grated potatoes, they are fried in butter with garlic, parsley and, in this recipe, crème fraîche, then cooked until a rich golden brown and crisp on both sides. They can be made as individual pancakes or one large pancake served cut into wedges.

1 Peel the potatoes and grate them into a mixing bowl.

2 Beat the eggs and add them to the bowl with the crème fraîche, garlic and parsley. Season with salt and pepper and mix everything together. Divide the mixture evenly into quarters.

3 Add 30g (1oz) of the butter to a small frying pan and melt over a medium heat. Pour in one-quarter of the mixture and cook for 10 minutes. Turn the pancake over using a spatula to cook for 10 minutes on the other side. The cooked pancake should be golden brown and very crisp. Remove it from the pan and keep warm.

4 Cook 3 more pancakes in the same way. Serve them sprinkled with chopped parsley to garnish, accompanied with grilled sausages and a green salad if you wish.

Puy Green Lentil Salad

SALADE DE LENTILLES VERTES DU PUY

Serves 6

Preparation time: 15 mins

Cooling time: 20 mins

Cooking time: 45 mins

Ingredients

400g (14oz) dried Puy green lentils

3 tablespoons duck fat (or lard)

1 large onion, sliced

50g (1¾oz) French cured ham, cut into small dice

1 bouquet garni

250g (9oz) smoked streaky bacon, cut into small dice

3 shallots, chopped

salt and freshly ground black pepper

chopped flat leaf parsley, to garnish

For the vinaigrette

1 tablespoon mustard

3 tablespoons wine vinegar of choice

135ml (4½fl oz) walnut oil

The lentils grown in the Le Puy region are grey-green in colour and are deemed to have a superior flavour to other varieties of lentil. Their other advantage is that they retain their shape and don't disintegrate after cooking, so can be served as an accompaniment to meat and fish dishes as well as in salads.

1 Rinse the lentils. Put them in a flameproof casserole and cover them with cold water. Bring to a boil, then immediately drain them.

2 Heat the duck fat (or lard) in the same casserole over a low heat. Fry the onion with the ham until golden. Add the lentils, twice their volume of water (or follow the instructions on the packet) and the bouquet garni. Season lightly with salt and pepper. Bring to simmering point and leave the surface of the water to ripple gently without it ever boiling hard. Cook the lentils for about 30 minutes until tender, then let them cool in their cooking liquid for about 20 minutes before draining, discarding the bouquet garni.

3 Fry the bacon in a dry frying pan until golden brown.

4 Make the vinaigrette. Whisk together the mustard, vinegar, oil and some pepper until emulsified. Pour over the still-warm lentils and add the bacon and shallots. Stir to coat the salad with the vinaigrette, then sprinkle with chopped flat leaf parsley to garnish and serve immediately.

Pot-roasted Veal with Walnuts

RÔTI DE VEAU FERMIER AUX NOIX

Serves 4

Preparation time: 20 mins

Cooking time: 1 hour 20 mins

Ingredients

30g (1oz) lard

1 boneless farm-reared (higher-welfare) veal roasting joint, preferably top rump or loin cut from the centre, weighing about 1kg (2lb 4oz), tied at regular intervals with thin string

2 shallots, finely sliced

2 carrots, cut into very small dice

1 onion, finely sliced

200ml (7fl oz) dry white wine

1 bouquet garni

100g (3½oz) walnut halves

150ml (5fl oz) crème fraîche

salt and freshly ground black pepper

Fresh pasta such as tagliatelle or rice both make good accompaniments to this pot-roasted veal or you could serve it with a fricassée of ceps when the mushrooms are in season.

1 Melt the lard in a flameproof casserole over a medium heat and sear the veal joint, turning it over regularly, until it is evenly browned on all sides.

2 Remove the veal from the casserole and add the shallots, carrots and onion. Fry for 2 minutes, stirring until the vegetables are very lightly coloured. Return the veal to the pan, add the wine and bouquet garni and season with salt and pepper. Cover the casserole and simmer for 1 hour, turning the veal joint over from time to time.

3 When the veal is cooked, remove it from the casserole and keep it hot, covered with foil.

4 Strain the cooking juices through a fine-mesh sieve, crushing the vegetables with a pestle to make a very concentrated sauce. Pour this back into the casserole. Crush the walnut halves using the pestle and mortar or grind them coarsely in a food processor and add to the casserole with the crème fraîche. Bring to the boil and adjust the seasoning, if necessary.

5 Cut the veal into slices. Arrange them on a serving plate and coat the slices with the walnut sauce. Serve immediately.

Bourbonnaise Chicken with White Wine

POULET BOURBONNAIS AU VIN BLANC

Serves 4–6

Preparation time: 30 mins

Cooking time: 1¼ hours

Ingredients

1 free-range chicken, weighing 1.6–1.8kg (3lb 8oz–4lb)

4 or 5 garlic cloves, unpeeled

3 tablespoons oil

1 tablespoon butter

1.2kg (2lb 10oz) carrots, chopped

2 tablespoons chopped fresh parsley

200ml (7fl oz) dry white wine

200ml (7fl oz) liquid crème fraîche (or unwhipped double cream)

salt and freshly ground black pepper

Bourbonnaise chickens are a hardy breed with white plumage flecked with black on their head, neck, wing tips and tail. They get their name from a former region of France to the north of the Massif Central, once ruled by the Bourbon family.

1 Preheat the oven to 200°C (400°F), Gas Mark 6. Stuff the cavity of the chicken with the garlic cloves. Season the outside and inside of the bird with salt and pepper.

2 Heat the oil and butter in a flameproof casserole and gradually brown the chicken on all sides over a medium heat.

3 When the chicken is golden brown, transfer it in the casserole to the oven and cook for about 1 hour, basting the chicken regularly with its cooking juices.

4 Meanwhile, cook the carrots in a saucepan of salted boiling water for 15–20 minutes or until they are just tender but remain a little firm. Drain and set aside.

5 When the chicken is cooked, remove it from the casserole. To check it is done, tilt the chicken to one side to see if the juices that run out are clear. It is ready when the juices are transparent without any traces of blood.

6 Cover the chicken with foil and leave it to rest while you finish cooking the carrots and sauce.

7 Add the carrots to the casserole and fry them until golden, then remove and sprinkle them with the chopped parsley. Transfer them to a serving dish and keep warm. Pour off the excess fat from the casserole. Add the wine and reduce it by half over a high heat. Whisk in the crème fraîche (or cream) and leave it to bubble gently until the sauce is thickened and glossy. Adjust the seasoning, if necessary.

8 Carve or joint the chicken, arranging the pieces on a serving dish. Serve the carrots and sauce separately.

Truffade

Serves 6	Preparation time: 30 mins	Cooking time: 50 mins

Ingredients

400g (14oz) fresh tomme

1.2kg (2lb 10oz) waxy salad potatoes, such as Charlotte

200g (7oz) smoked streaky bacon

6 tablespoons lard

2 garlic cloves, chopped

salt and freshly ground black pepper

A classic dish originating from Cantal in the Auvergne, this requires few ingredients, the main one being potatoes, which are sliced, sautéed in a frying pan with streaky bacon lardons and pressed down to make a type of galette, before topping with fresh tomme cheese that melts into them. Fresh tomme is a hard cows' milk cheese produced in the Aubrac and Cantal regions of the Massif Central. If you are unable to find it, Gruyère or a young Cantal can be used instead.

1 Cut the fresh tomme into thin slices and set aside. Peel and slice the potatoes into thin rounds.

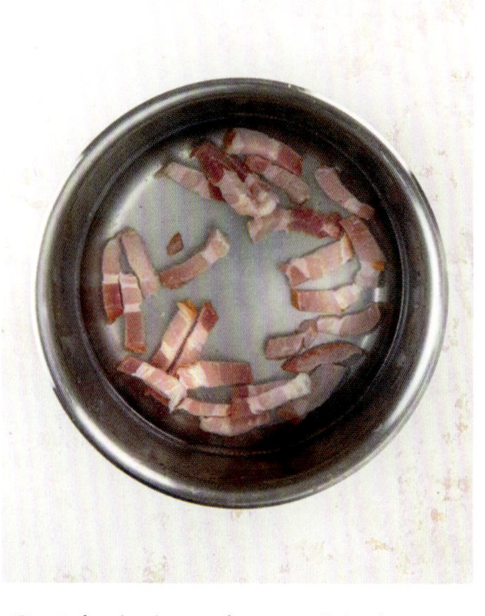

2 Snip the bacon into small lardons. Put them in a saucepan, cover with cold water and bring to a boil, then drain.

3 Heat 2 tablespoons of the lard in a large, heavy-based frying pan and fry the bacon lardons until golden brown. Drain and set aside.

4 Add the remaining lard to the frying pan, and when it sizzles, add the potato slices.

Worth knowing

The potato reigns supreme in the Auvergne where it is a called *trufada* or *truffa* in the local dialect, from which the name of this dish derives.

5 Spread the potato slices out evenly into a layer about 4cm (1½ inches) thick. Fry over a medium heat until they turn golden, shaking the pan from time to time to avoid them sticking. Do not stir them, as they need to form into a kind of potato pancake.

6 When the underside is golden brown, cover with a lid or heatproof plate that is smaller than your saucepan and add a heavy weight on top.

7 Lower the heat and leave the potatoes to cook very gently for about 30 minutes. Halfway through the cooking time, remove the weight and lid or plate and add the bacon lardons and garlic. Season with salt and pepper.

8 When the potatoes are cooked through, cover them with the cheese slices in a single layer.

9 Using a fork, gently lift the potato slices so that the cheese can melt down into the middle.

10 Place the lid or plate and weight on top again and cook over a very low heat for 1–2 minutes – the time the cheese will take to melt. When you hear a gentle sizzling sound, remove from the heat and turn the *truffade* out on to a hot serving plate.

Auvergne Pot-roasted Pork

POTÉE AUVERGNATE

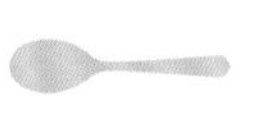

Serves 8 | **Preparation time: 30 mins** | **Cooking time: 3 hours**

Ingredients

500g (1lb 2oz) smoked pork belly

1 pork shoulder

10 black peppercorns

2 cloves

1 onion

2 garlic cloves, peeled

1 bouquet garni

800g (1lb 2oz) carrots

800g (1lb 12oz) potatoes

3 turnips (or other root vegetable)

4 leeks, trimmed and cleaned

1 round cabbage

1 French poaching sausage (*saucisson à cuire*)

salt (if needed) and freshly ground black pepper

This rustic pot-roast recipe from the Auvergne combines pork belly and shoulder of pork with root vegetables and cabbage. In France, both cuts of pork used here would be *demi-sel*, or lightly salt-cured, which isn't readily available elsewhere, but using smoked pork belly with fresh pork shoulder makes an acceptable, more accessible substitute. Long, slow cooking in a single pan ensures the meat is succulent and deliciously tender.

1 Put the pork belly and shoulder in a large flameproof casserole and pour cold water over them to cover. Bring to the boil, skim the foam and leave to boil for 5 minutes. Drain the meats and pour the water away.

2 Return the meats to the casserole and cover with fresh cold water. Bring to the boil and skim the foam from the surface before adding the peppercorns. Stick the cloves into the onion and add to the casserole with the garlic cloves and bouquet garni. Cover and leave to simmer gently for 1½ hours.

3 Meanwhile, peel all the root vegetables, then cut the carrots in half lengthways if large and the turnips (or other root vegetable) and potatoes into quarters if large. Tie the leeks together in bundles with kitchen string.

4 Remove the coarse outer leaves of the cabbage, cut it into quarters and remove the core. Blanch the cabbage quarters in a saucepan of salted boiling water for 3 minutes. Drain and refresh under cold running water, then set aside.

5 After the meats have been cooking for 1½ hours, add the cabbage quarters, leek bundles, carrots and turnips (or other root vegetable). Simmer for another 1 hour.

6 Prick the sausage with a fork so that it does not burst while cooking. Add to the casserole with the potatoes and cook for about 30 minutes. Season with pepper but taste before adding any salt, as the pork belly may have made it salty enough. Drain the meats, sausage and vegetables and serve in a large shallow dish.

Aligot Potatoes

ALIGOT

Serves 6 | **Preparation time: 30 mins** | **Cooking time: 30–40 mins**

Ingredients

1kg (2lb 4oz) floury potatoes, unpeeled

100g (3½oz) butter, softened

250–300ml (9–10fl oz) crème fraîche

1 garlic clove, crushed

500g (1lb 2oz) fresh Tome de Laguiole, thinly sliced

salt

***Aligot* is a potato dish from the Aubrac region in the south-central Massif Central. Fresh tomme cheese, butter and crème fraîche are gradually beaten into mashed potatoes until they reach a smooth, elastic consistency. Outside of the area where it is produced, fresh tomme is very difficult to find. While irreplaceable when the dish is made in the Aubrac and where it is so stretchy it is sometimes cut with scissors to serve, fresh Cantal tomme could be used or equal quantities of cooking mozzarella and Gruyère.**

1 Wash the potatoes thoroughly and cook them in their skins in a saucepan of boiling water for 20–30 minutes until they are tender.

2 Drain the potatoes and peel off their skins while still warm. Pass them through a potato ricer or the finest perforated disc of a vegetable mill into a bowl. Gradually beat in the butter and the crème fraîche until you have a smooth and thick yet supple purée. Add the garlic and season lightly with salt.

3 Transfer the purée to a saucepan over a gentle heat. Add all the cheese in one go, mixing vigorously with a wooden spatula but, rather than stirring it round and round, lifting the purée from underneath. Keep beating continuously and vigorously until the purée drops off in a stretchy, very smooth ribbon when you lift the spatula. Serve immediately or the cheese will break down and become granular.

Hazelnut Cake

GÂTEAU AUX NOISETTES

Serves 6

Preparation time: 30 mins

Cooking time: 45 mins

Ingredients

100g (3½oz) hazelnuts (preferably fresh), skinned – see Tip

180g (6¼oz) plain flour

1½ teaspoons baking powder

3 eggs

180g (6¼oz) sugar

150g (5½oz) butter, softened, plus extra for greasing

pinch of salt

This cake is a variation of the *Creusois*, a light, hazelnut-flavoured sponge that is a speciality of Aubusson in the Creuse department. According to legend, the recipe was discovered on a parchment dating from the 15th century that was found in the ruins of a monastery near the medieval town of Crocq, also in Creuse.

1 Preheat the oven to 170°C (325°F), Gas Mark 3. Grease a 22cm (8½-inch) round cake tin with butter. Coarsely chop the hazelnuts in a food processor. Sift together the flour and baking powder.

2 Separate the eggs. Whisk the egg yolks with the sugar and butter in a mixing bowl until evenly combined, then fold in the flour and baking powder and the chopped hazelnuts.

3 Whisk the egg whites with the salt in another mixing bowl until they are standing in stiff peaks. Stir 1 tablespoon of the whisked whites into the cake batter until incorporated and then lightly fold in the rest with a spatula.

4 Transfer the cake batter to the cake tin and bake for 45 minutes or until a skewer inserted into the centre of the cake comes out clean. Cool the cake in the tin before turning out on to a wire rack.

Tip

If your hazelnuts are fresh, soak them in boiling water for 30 seconds before removing their skins and then dry them out in the oven for a few minutes, without letting them brown.

EACH REGION
HAS ITS OWN SWEET TREATS!

La Vie en Rose

Go to Champagne for the pink biscuits of Reims, once served as an accompaniment to the region's other great speciality, their famous tiny bubbles in a glass. Something that makes the biscuit special, apart from its colour, is that it is cooked twice, or, as the French say, *bis-cuit*! According to the baker who created the recipe, the characteristic pink colour only came about by accident. He added carmine, a vegetable dye, to the second batch of dough he was baking in an attempt to mask the black dots from the vanilla pod he had added to flavour the first batch of white biscuit dough. Light and crisp, the pink biscuit of Reims is traditionally eaten dipped in a glass of wine, port or champagne, but it can be enjoyed in many other ways, notably as a base for cakes and desserts made with soaked biscuits, such as a charlotte or tiramisu. They are enough to give your desserts a rosy glow!

A Brioche to Brag About

One thing that's certain is the people of the Vendée did not wait for Marie-Antoinette to suggest they eat brioche, as they were already doing so! In fact, it is the tradition that the Gâche de Vendée, a type of oval sweet, yeasted bread that is golden brown and scored on top, has been served in the region at different festivals and celebrations such as marriages, baptisms and Easter since the Middle Ages and from 2011 onwards has benefited from IGP certification. Butter-based, the brioche dough also contains crème fraîche, which enhances its fresh dairy flavour. This very soft brioche is equally good eaten plain or served spread with butter or jam.

Time to Get out Your Preserving Pans!

The delicious Itxassou cherry jam makes a sublime accompaniment to Tomme de Brebis cheese, a Basque Cake (see recipe page 186) or to spread generously on to buttered bread slices. To make a genuine Itxassou cherry jam, however, you must use only the Basque Country's local varieties of cherry: Peloa, Xapata and Beltxa. Cultivation of these was revived by a group of growers at the end of the 1980s around the village of Itxassou, which has since made this jam its speciality, much to the delight of the region's gourmets!

A Cake with its Own Museum

First made in the middle of the 19th century in the town of Cambo-les-Bains, the Basque Cake, as you've probably already guessed, is one of the great specialities of the Basque Country. This is a sweet tart, which has a shortcrust pastry case filled with jam or custard (see recipe page 186). The cake became such an institution in the region that a museum has been dedicated to it at Sare (also in the Pyrénées-Atlantiques department), where you can discover the secrets of how it is made and even take part in a patisserie workshop to learn how to prepare it yourself.

A Boat-shaped Sweet Biscuit

Pastis, soap and a distinctive accent are just some of the local specialities for which Marseille is famous. But have you heard of the Marseille navette? This small dry biscuit, flavoured with orange flower water, takes its name and shape from the small boat that carried Mary Magdalene, her brother Lazarus and her sister Martha into Marseille's old port in the 1st century AD. The bakery where the biscuit was invented in 1781, Le Four des Navettes, still exists and each year at Candlemas it welcomes the archbishop of Marseille who comes to bless this delicious little biscuit. You would be crazy not to try it!

Corsican Nectar

The tradition of beekeeping in Corsica, which dates back to ancient times, has today been recognized at national and European level with the award of AOC and AOP certification for the six types of honey made on the so-called Island of Beauty. This success is due to the Corsican ecotype bee, *Apis mellifera mellifera* (western honey bee). A genuine star of the bee world, it stands apart from its peers due to its ability to adapt completely to the island's climate, allowing a sustainable, reliable cultivation of honey and the production of a very high-quality product. The bees are extremely closely protected in the areas where they live to ensure their conservation. However, they also have the chance of a regular change of scenery thanks to the beekeepers moving their hives according to the seasons to take advantage of making different honey using every type of Corsican flower.

Encalat Curd Tart

TARTE À L'ENCALAT

Serves 6

Preparation time: 30 mins

Resting time: at least 2 hours

Cooking time: 55 mins

Ingredients

For the pastry

150g (5½oz) butter, softened, plus extra for greasing

¼ teaspoon salt

1 teaspoon sugar

1 egg

1 tablespoon milk

170g (6oz) plain flour, plus extra for dusting

For the filling

500g (1lb 2oz) fromage blanc (or use ricotta)

3 eggs

100g (3½oz) sugar

1 tablespoon orange flower water

finely grated zest of 1 orange (optional), plus fine shreds to decorate

1 teaspoon salt

This dessert, which is traditionally made with sour/curdled cows' milk, is unique to the northern part of the Aveyron. In the south of the department, the same tart is made with a fresh soft cheese called Brousse de Brebis and is similarly perfumed with orange flower water. This tart, known traditionally as *flaune* or *flône*, is served at all regional celebrations.

1 First make the pastry. Work the butter with a spatula in a mixing bowl until it is very soft and creamy. Add the salt, sugar, egg and milk, beating until all the ingredients are combined. When the mixture is smooth, gradually add the flour, mixing in each addition before you add the next. Work the mixture as little as possible to make a dough. Shape it into a ball, wrap in greaseproof paper and leave it to rest for at least 2 hours in the refrigerator.

2 Preheat the oven to 200°C (400°F), Gas Mark 6. Grease a 24cm (9½-inch) round flan tin with butter. Roll out the pastry and use it to line the tin. Line the pastry case with greaseproof paper and fill it with baking beans, then bake blind for 15 minutes. Remove the baking beans and greaseproof paper and bake for another 5 minutes. Remove the pastry case from the oven and leave it to cool.

3 Whisk the filling ingredients together in a mixing bowl until very smooth and quite runny. Pour the filling into the pastry case, return it to the oven at the same temperature and bake for about 35 minutes until the filling has the consistency of a crème caramel. Remove the tart from the oven and leave it to cool. Serve with fine shreds of orange zest sprinkled over to decorate.

'Scalded' Biscuits

ÉCHAUDÉS

Serves 8–10 | **Preparation time: 45 mins** | **Resting time: 12 hours** | **Cooking time: 40 mins**

Ingredients

500g (1lb 2oz) plain flour, plus extra for dusting

½ teaspoon salt

2 eggs, beaten

10g (¼oz) aniseed

100g (3½oz) butter, cut into small pieces

about 200ml (7fl oz) warm milk

These biscuits take their unusual name from the dough being 'scalded' in boiling water before it is baked. Flavoured with aniseed, they are popular all over the Aveyron, particularly in the Ségala region that straddles Aveyron and the Tarn departments.

1 The day before, sift the flour and salt into a mixing bowl. Make a well in the centre and add the eggs, aniseed and butter. Rub the ingredients together with your fingertips, drawing the flour into the centre. Gradually add just enough warm milk to make a very firm dough, then knead it vigorously for about 15 minutes. Roll the dough into a ball, wrap it in a clean tea towel and leave to rest overnight or for 12 hours in the refrigerator.

2 The next day, roll out the dough on a lightly floured work surface until about 8mm (⅜ inch) thick and cut it into triangles with 10cm (4-inch) sides. Fold the points of the triangles inwards one over the other to create small tricorn hat shapes.

3 Bring a large pan of water to the boil and add the triangles, a few at a time. Remove them with a skimmer as soon as they rise to the surface of the water. Drain them on kitchen paper. Line several baking sheets with nonstick baking paper and line up the boiled triangles in rows on them.

4 Preheat the oven to 220°C (425°F), Gas Mark 7. Bake the biscuits in batches for about 20 minutes until they are just golden. Leave them to cool. These can be stored in an airtight container for several days.

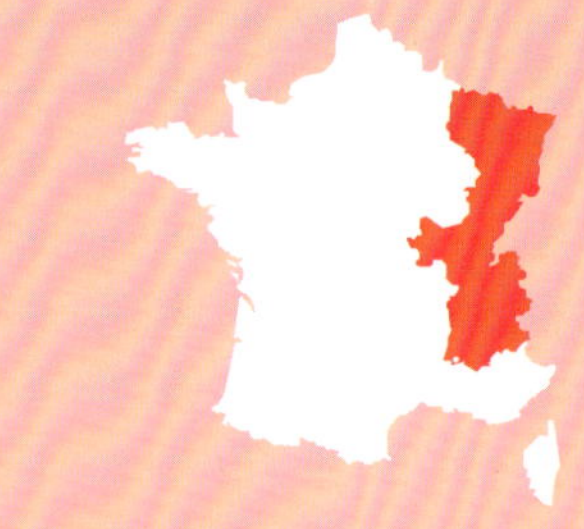

Eastern France

AND THE ALPS

Quiche Lorraine

Serves 4–6

Preparation time: 25 mins

Resting time: 30 mins

Cooking time: 50–55 mins

Ingredients

For the shortcrust pastry

225g (8oz) plain flour, plus extra for dusting

2 pinches of salt

150g (5½oz) butter, cut into very small pieces

For the filling

200g (7oz) smoked bacon lardons

5 eggs

400ml (14fl oz) crème fraîche

freshly grated nutmeg

salt and freshly ground black pepper

This savoury tart from the Lorraine region was traditionally filled only with eggs, crème fraîche and bacon lardons baked in a shortcrust pastry case. During the mid-20th century, its popularity spread widely, both across France and to other countries, including the UK and USA, where cooks began adding cheese to the filling, but this is still considered to be inauthentic.

1 First make the pastry. Sift the flour into a mixing bowl, make a well in the centre and add the salt, followed by the butter. Rub the ingredients together with your fingertips and then gradually add enough cold water, 1 tablespoon at a time (you will need to add about 8 tablespoons in total), mixing to combine the ingredients and then working quickly until you have a very soft, pliable dough.

2 Spread out the dough on a floured work surface, pressing it and pushing it away from you with the palm of your hand but without kneading it too much. Shape the dough into a ball and flatten it. Wrap it in greaseproof paper and leave it to rest for 30 minutes in the refrigerator.

3 Preheat the oven to 200°C (400°F), Gas Mark 6.

4 Roll out the dough on a lightly floured work surface until 4mm (about ⅛ inch) thick and use it to line a 26cm (10½-inch) loose-bottomed flan tin. Prick the dough all over with a fork and line with nonstick baking paper. Fill with baking beans and bake blind for 10 minutes. Remove the beans and baking paper and leave to cool.

5 Prepare the filling. Fry the bacon lardons very lightly in a nonstick frying pan, then drain. Spread them over the pastry base.

6 Beat the eggs and crème fraîche together, then season with salt, pepper and a little freshly grated nutmeg. Pour into the pastry case over the lardons.

7 Bake the quiche for 35–40 minutes. Remove it from the oven and serve hot with a green salad.

Onion and Bacon Pizza

FLAMMENKÜCHE

Serves 4 (Makes 2) | Preparation time: 30 mins | Resting time: 1 hour | Cooking time: 15–20 mins

Ingredients

For the dough

400g (14oz) plain flour, plus extra for dusting
pinch of salt
10g (¼oz) fast-action dried yeast
5 tablespoons groundnut oil

For the topping

2–3 tablespoons groundnut oil
2 medium onions, finely sliced
200g (7oz) smoked streaky bacon, rinded
200ml (7oz) crème fraîche

***Flammenküche*, from Alsace, translates literally as 'baked in the flames'. Similar to pizzas, authentic *Flammenküche* are cooked in a wood-fired bread oven and eaten hot in *winstubs* (wine bars serving food). If you have a pizza oven at home, you can use this, but if using a conventional oven, it is important to roll the dough as thinly as possible (it must be almost transparent) and to have the oven turned up to maximum heat.**

1 First make the dough. Sift the flour and salt into a mixing bowl, crumble in the yeast and stir to mix. Make a well in the centre and pour in the oil and 200ml (7fl oz) water, then mix together, gradually drawing the flour towards the centre of the bowl. Using your hands, knead for a few minutes until you have a smooth, flexible dough. Cover the bowl with a clean tea towel and leave to rest for 1 hour in the refrigerator.

2 Meanwhile, prepare the topping. Heat the oil in a frying pan and fry the onions over a gentle heat until they are transparent. Cut the bacon into very thin strips, place them in a saucepan of cold water and bring to the boil, then drain.

3 Preheat the oven to its highest setting. Divide the dough in half and roll out each half on a lightly floured work surface as thinly as possible into a circle. Line 2 baking sheets with nonstick baking paper. Lift each dough circle on to a lined baking sheet by carefully wrapping each one around the rolling pin and then unrolling on to the sheet. Dampen the dough all over by brushing lightly with water, then lift and roll over the edges to form a flat border all round. Prick the dough all over with a fork. Spread half the crème fraîche over each one, followed by half the onions and half the bacon. Bake for 10–15 minutes until the edges of the pizzas are golden brown. Serve immediately.

Roast Pork with Quetsche Plums

RÔTI DE PORC AUX QUETSCHES

Serves 6

Preparation time: 30 mins

Cooking time: 1¼ hours

Ingredients

50g (1¾oz) butter

1 pork loin joint, weighing 1.5kg (3lb 5oz), chined (see Tip)

1 green cabbage

50g (1¾oz) lard

50g (1¾oz) brown sugar

1kg (2lb 4oz) Quetsche plums, stoned

salt and freshly ground black pepper

This sweet-sour recipe owes its roots to German cuisine. If you want the roast pork to taste a little sweeter, dust it with brown sugar before putting it in the oven so that the sugar caramelizes on the surface of the meat as it roasts. Quetsche plums from Alsace are small and oval-shaped with dark purple skins. They have juicy orange flesh and make an excellent accompaniment to roast pork.

1 Preheat the oven to 180°C (350°F), Gas Mark 4. Use some of the butter to grease a large ovenproof dish. Place the pork in the dish and season with salt and pepper. Cut the rest of the butter into small pieces, spread it over the pork and roast it for 1¼ hours. Halfway through the roasting time, cover the pork with foil.

2 Meanwhile, remove any damaged outer leaves from the cabbage and cut it into quarters. Blanch it for 5 minutes in a saucepan of lightly salted boiling water, then drain. Melt the lard in a flameproof casserole over a low heat. Add the cabbage, cover the casserole and cook for about 20 minutes, uncovering about halfway through cooking so that liquid from the cabbage can evaporate.

3 Dissolve the sugar in 200ml (7fl oz) water in a saucepan, then add the plums and cook them gently until they are tender and well caramelized but not falling apart.

4 Transfer the pork to a hot serving dish and surround it with the plums and cabbage. Cut the pork into individual chops between the bones and serve immediately.

Tip

Ask a butcher to chine the joint for you: this means loosening the bone, but leaving it attached. Cooking the joint on the bone ensures you get maximum flavour.

Alsatian Meat and Potato Casserole

BAEKENOFE

Serves 6–8 | **Preparation time: 20 mins** | **Marinating time: 12 hours** | **Cooking time: 4 hours**

Ingredients

500g (1lb 2oz) mutton shoulder

500g (1lb 2oz) pork shoulder

500g (1lb 2oz) braising beef (topside or chuck steak)

5 large onions

2 garlic cloves

3 cloves, crushed

500ml (18fl oz) dry Alsace white wine

1 bouquet garni

200g (7oz) plain flour

1kg (2lb 4oz) potatoes

30g (1oz) lard

salt and freshly ground black pepper

This slow-cooked Alsatian stew is made with different meats – mutton, pork and beef in this recipe – and potatoes. Accompany it with a crisp green salad.

1. The day before, cut the meats into large cubes. Peel 2 of the onions and stick the cloves into them. Put the meats, clove-studded onions and garlic into a dish and add the wine and bouquet garni. Season with a little salt and pepper, cover and leave to marinate overnight or for 12 hours in the refrigerator.
2. The next day, sift the flour into a mixing bowl, add 100ml (3½fl oz) cold water and mix to make a smooth dough.
3. Preheat the oven to 160°C (325°F), Gas Mark 3. Peel the potatoes and the remaining 3 onions and slice them into rounds.
4. Grease a casserole with the lard and put a layer of potato slices in the bottom, followed by a layer of the mixed meats (reserve the marinade) and a layer of sliced onions. Continue these layers, seasoning with salt and pepper between each layer, until all the ingredients are used up, finishing with a layer of potatoes.
5. Remove the bouquet garni and the clove-studded onions from the marinade and add the marinade to the casserole. The liquid must be level with the top layer of potatoes. If it is not, add a little water to top it up.
6. Roll the dough into a long thin sausage and press this around the rim of the casserole. Put the lid on top and press it down into the dough to seal the casserole (this is to prevent steam escaping during cooking).
7. Cook in the oven for 4 hours and serve straight from the casserole.

Sauerkraut

CHOUCROUTE

Preparation time: 30 mins	Serves 6	Cooking time: about 1 hour 40 mins

80g (3oz) goose fat (or lard)

salt and freshly ground black pepper

300ml (10fl oz) dry Alsace white wine (Riesling or Pinot Blanc)

4 or 5 coriander seeds

1 clove

1 garlic clove

600g (1lb 5oz) pork collar

400g (14oz) smoked back bacon

1 bay leaf

10 juniper berries

2 large onions, sliced

1 salted pork shank

6 Strasbourg sausages
3 smoked Montbéliard sausages

1.5kg (3lb 5oz) raw sauerkraut

6 potatoes

Ingredients

1.5kg (3lb 5oz) raw sauerkraut

4 or 5 coriander seeds

1 clove

1 salted pork shank (or use unsmoked gammon shank)

400g (14oz) smoked back bacon

600g (1lb 5oz) pork collar

80g (3oz) goose fat (or lard)

2 onions, sliced

1 garlic clove, crushed

10 juniper berries

1 bay leaf

300ml (10fl oz) dry Alsace white wine (Riesling or Pinot Blanc)

6 potatoes, washed but not peeled

6 Strasbourg sausages (or use frankfurters)

3 smoked Montbéliard sausages

salt and freshly ground black pepper

***Choucroute* (the French term for sauerkraut) in Alsace comes with an array of charcuterie and is flavoured with juniper berries and the local white wine. Montbéliard is a traditional French sausage with a rich brown colour. Smoking it over sawdust gives it a unique flavour. Strasbourg sausages, originally from the city of that name, are the French version of frankfurters.**

1 Wash the raw sauerkraut several times in cold water. Drain it and then press it in a sieve to extract all the water.

2 Tie up the coriander seeds and clove in a small square of muslin so that the spices can be easily removed before serving.

3 To cook the meats, first put the shank in a saucepan of cold water and bring to the boil. Simmer gently for 30–40 minutes and then add the other meats. Cook for another 1 hour, still over a gentle heat. Remove the pan from the heat and leave the meats to sit in their cooking juices.

4 Preheat the oven to 180°C (350°F), Gas Mark 4. Heat the goose fat (or lard) in a large flameproof casserole or ovenproof pan over a medium heat and fry the onions and garlic until softened and browned.

5 Add the sauerkraut, juniper berries, bay leaf and spices. Pour in the wine and some of the cooking liquid from the meats. Season lightly with salt and continue cooking on the hob until the liquid is simmering. Cover the casserole, transfer to the oven and cook for 1½ hours, adding more liquid from time to time if it evaporates too quickly.

6 About 30 minutes before the end of the sauerkraut cooking time, cook the unpeeled potatoes in a saucepan of salted boiling water for 20–30 minutes, depending on their size, until tender.

7 A few minutes before the sauerkraut is ready, poach the sausages in a saucepan of simmering water, without letting the water boil as this may cause the sausages to burst. Gently reheat the meats in their cooking liquid.

8 Remove the casserole from the oven and taste and adjust the seasoning, adding salt and pepper as necessary. Transfer the sauerkraut, meats and sausages to a large hot serving platter. Accompany with the potatoes.

Chicken with Vin Jaune and Morels

COQ AU VIN JAUNE ET AUX MORILLES

Serves 8

Preparation time: 30 mins

Cooking time: 55 mins

Ingredients

1 chicken (traditionally a young cockerel from Bresse), weighing about 2kg (4lb 8oz)

300g (10½oz) fresh morels

3 tablespoons plain flour

60g (2¼oz) butter

300ml (10fl oz) *vin jaune*

750ml (1⅓ pints) crème fraîche

salt and freshly ground black pepper

Vin jaune **(meaning 'yellow wine' in French) is a speciality of the mountainous Jura region of eastern France. The wine is matured in a barrel under a film of yeast and has a similar flavour to dry fino sherry. If you cannot find** ***vin jaune*****, you can replace it with 100ml (3½fl oz) of dry sherry and 200ml (7fl oz) Chardonnay wine.**

1 Cut the chicken into 8 pieces. Trim off the woody ends of the morel stems and clean them thoroughly (see Tip).

2 Preheat the oven to 180°C (350°F), Gas Mark 4. Season the chicken pieces with salt and pepper and dust them lightly with the flour. Heat the butter in a flameproof casserole over a gentle heat and fry the chicken pieces on all sides without letting them colour. Cover the casserole and cook in the oven for about 40 minutes.

3 Remove the casserole from the oven, pour off the fat and deglaze with the *vin jaune*. Whisk in the crème fraîche until incorporated, turning the chicken pieces over several times, and then add the morels. Put the casserole on the hob and leave it to simmer gently, uncovered, until the sauce thickens enough to coat the back of a spoon. Taste and adjust the seasoning, if necessary. Transfer the chicken pieces and morels to a hot serving dish and pour over the sauce. Serve immediately.

Tip

The deep, honeycomb-like cavities covering the morels must be thoroughly cleaned to remove any grit that can become trapped in them. Use a small brush to do this, rinsing the morels as little as possible in order to better preserve their delicate aroma.

STAUB
STAUB

Dombes-style Sautéed Frogs' Legs

CUISSES DE GRENOUILLES DE LA DOMBES SAUTÉES

Serves 4 | **Preparation time: 20 mins** | **Soaking time: 1 hour** | **Cooking time: 6–8 mins**

Ingredients

48 frogs' legs

distilled white vinegar, for rinsing

cold milk

1 garlic clove, finely chopped

2 tablespoons chopped flat leaf parsley

plain flour, for dusting

300g (10½oz) butter (preferably clarified – see Tip)

salt and freshly ground black pepper

Frogs' legs have been a popular dish in France since medieval times. Those from the frogs on the marshland of the Dombes region in the Ain department are highly prized and, to protect the species, gathering them is now very strictly controlled.

1 Cut off the ends of the frogs' legs with kitchen scissors. Rinse the frogs' legs in cold water with white vinegar added and then soak them in a large bowl filled with cold milk for 1 hour. Drain and carefully blot them with kitchen paper. Mix the garlic and parsley together.

2 Dust the frogs' legs with flour, gently wiping them to remove the excess, as they should only be coated with a fine layer.

3 Place 2 large frying pans over a high heat and melt 50g (1¾oz) of the butter in each. Add the frogs' legs, placing them well apart, and season with salt and pepper. As soon as they start to turn golden, turn the frogs' legs over one at a time and lower the heat under the pans. Continue to cook them gently until they are golden on both sides.

4 Transfer the frogs' legs to 4 hot serving bowls and pour the butter from the frying pans over them. Melt the remaining butter in a separate pan over a low heat. As soon as it melts and foams, pour equal amounts over the bowls. Sprinkle with the garlic and parsley mixture and serve immediately.

Tip

Although this dish is very simple, it needs to be prepared with care. The cooking requires particularly close attention, as the flesh of the frogs' legs must not dry out and the butter must not burn. To avoid the latter, it is best to use clarified butter.

Comté Cheese Fondue

FONDUE COMTOISE

Serves 4

Preparation time: 10 mins

Cooking time: 15 mins

Ingredients

1 garlic clove, peeled

10g (¼oz) potato flour

3–4 tablespoons kirsch

400ml (14fl oz) dry white wine (preferably Arbois Chardonnay)

400g (14oz) Comté cheese, thinly sliced

400g (14oz) Emmental cheese, thinly sliced

country bread, cut into small cubes

freshly ground black pepper

In medieval times, when people of the mountainous region of Franche-Comté adopted neighbouring Switzerland's Emmental cheese, it was inevitable that fondue would follow. In this recipe, as well as Emmental, Comté cheese is added and, of course, Arbois wine from the Jura.

1 Rub the garlic clove over the inside of a fondue pot. Stir the potato flour into the kirsch until smooth.

2 Pour the wine into the fondue pot and heat it gently. When bubbles start to appear on the surface (the wine must be hot but not boiling), drop in the cheese slices, stirring continuously with a wooden spoon. When all the cheese has melted, add the kirsch mixture and mix well. Season with pepper.

3 Put the fondue burner in the centre of the table, place the pot on top and keep the heat low. Serve the bread cubes with the fondue. Each diner spears a cube of bread on a fondue fork and dips it into the cheese, turning the fork as they lift it out to avoid thin strands of cheese dripping off.

CHEESES
WITH A UNIQUE LOCAL FLAVOUR

Welcome to Camembert

Normandy is famous for its soft cheeses, such as Neufchâtel or Pont L'Évêque, but without doubt the most well known is Normandy Camembert. It stands apart from other Camemberts due to its AOC and AOP classifications, which ensure its manufacturing process is carried out according to very strict guidelines. It can only be made using selected raw Normandy cows' milk and it must be ladled by hand into moulds on a table. Five scoops from a special ladle, added 40–50 minutes apart, are needed to produce a Normandy Camembert and it also must be made within a clearly defined area covering just over 1,500 communes in the departments of the Orne, Calvados, Manche and part of the Eure. All these regulations make it superior to other Camemberts not bearing the Normandy label, and once you have tasted the genuine article you will have to admit that there is no comparison!

Put the Brie in Brilliant!

Brie de Meaux is a soft French cheese with a bloomy rind made from raw cows' milk, usually from the Île-de-France breed of cattle. Originally from the town of Meaux, located about 50 kilometres (30 miles) to the east of Paris, it is considered one of France's most emblematic cheeses. It has been protected with AOC classification since 1980, meaning only cheeses produced in the Meaux region and made following strict production regulations can bear the name, thereby guaranteeing its authenticity and superior quality. Without doubt, it will make a *brie-lliant* cheeseboard.

Breakfast Cheese, Please!

While it might be traditional for locals in the regions of northern France to spread Maroilles on bread and dunk it in their bowl of chicory coffee at breakfast time, there is no obligation to follow this rather challenging custom in order to fully enjoy the cheese. Originally from Thiérache, Maroilles is a soft *pavé* cheese *(pavé* meaning 'paving stone', a reference to its shape) with a orange rind. As well as being a famous morning feast, it is used in many northern French recipes, such as *flamiche* (made with leeks) and *goyère* (a cheese tart with a brioche crust) or in a variation of Welsh rarebit instead of Cheddar. Its pungent smell and full-bodied flavour go well with a Flanders beer, assuming of course you would rather have an aperitif than breakfast.

J'adore Chaource!

Chaource is a small, cylindrical barrel-shaped AOC cows' milk cheese named after a village in the Aube department in the Grand Est region. It has a creamy melting texture, a mild, fruity, slightly acidic flavour and a white rind patterned with small red dots. It pairs well with both red and white wine, and could be an excuse for a glass of fine champagne.

A Pungent Alsatian Speciality

There is no denying it, Munster, or Munster-Géromé from the Vosges mountains of Alsace, is the cheese that has by far the strongest and most distinctive smell in France – to put it mildly! However, if you can brace yourself to get past this onslaught on your nostrils, you will be pleasantly surprised by its intense, slightly salty flavour and creamy melting texture, which are well worth stopping for a few moments to appreciate. As with many French cheeses, Munster is AOC-protected, which guarantees it is made using defined traditional methods and its unique and authentic flavour. If you are looking for a powerful and memorable sensory experience, you now know which cheese to choose!

Savoyard Tartiflette

TARTIFLETTE SAVOYARDE

Serves 4

Preparation time: 30 mins

Cooking time: 50–55 mins

Ingredients

600g (1lb 5oz) firm-fleshed potatoes

250g (9oz) farmhouse Reblochon cheese

1 tablespoon groundnut oil

200g (7oz) smoked bacon lardons

1 onion, thinly sliced

300ml (10fl oz) unwhipped double cream

Savoy is, without doubt, the region of France that boasts the greatest number of recipes using potatoes or *tartifles* as they are called there.

1 Rinse the potatoes. Cook them in a saucepan of boiling water for 20 minutes or until tender. Drain and refresh the potatoes under cold running water, then slice them.

2 Cut the Reblochon cheese in half horizontaly, then cut each half vertically to create four half-moons.

3 Heat the oil in a frying pan over a medium heat and fry the bacon lardons until browned.

4 Preheat the oven to 180°C (350°F), Gas Mark 4. Layer the sliced potatoes, lardons and onions in a large gratin dish. Cover with three of the Reblochon quarters with the rind facing downwards.

5 Heat the cream with the remaining Reblochon quarter in a saucepan over a low heat, mixing thoroughly to melt the cheese, then pour the mixture into the dish.

6 Bake for 25–30 minutes. Serve immediately, accompanied with a green salad.

Tip

If you prefer, you can fry the onions with the bacon lardons for 5 minutes so that they are lightly coloured.

Savoyard Crozets

CROZETS

Serves 6

Preparation time: 30 mins

Cooking time: 35 mins

Ingredients

3 medium potatoes, washed but unpeeled

300g (10½oz) type '00' soft wheat flour, plus extra for dusting

200g (7oz) buckwheat flour

4 eggs

1 teaspoon walnut oil

large knob of butter

salt

Crozets are a small, flat, square-shaped pasta traditionally made in the Savoy region using buckwheat or wheat flour, and sometimes a combination of the two, as in this recipe.

1. The day before, cook the potatoes in a saucepan of salted boiling water for about 30 minutes until tender. Drain and set them aside.

2. The next day, peel the potatoes and pass them through a vegetable mill fitted with the finest sieve. Put the potato mash in a large mixing bowl, add the flours and mix well. Add the eggs, one at a time, working the mixture continuously, then add just enough cold water to make a smooth but very dense dough. Add the oil and knead until the dough is very pliable.

3. If the quantity of dough is too big to handle, divide it into 2 or 3 pieces. Roll the pieces of dough on a lightly floured surface into large rectangles 3–4mm (about ⅛ inch) thick. Cut them into strips about 8mm (⅜ inch) wide, then cut the strips into small squares.

4. Cook the crozets in the same way as other fresh pasta in a large saucepan of salted boiling water for 5 minutes. Drain them and serve in a shallow dish topped with the butter.

Tip

When served as an accompaniment to a meat dish, crozets are frequently prepared as a gratin. To do this, grease an ovenproof gratin dish with butter and fill it with layers of crozets and grated cheese. Add a ladleful of stock and bake in a moderate oven until the top is golden.

Gratin Dauphinois

Serves 4–6

Preparation time: 15 mins

Cooking time: 55 mins

Ingredients

1kg (2lb 4oz) firm-fleshed potatoes
2 garlic cloves, peeled
80g (3oz) butter, softened
150g (5½oz) Emmental cheese, grated
freshly grated nutmeg
500ml (18fl oz) milk
250ml (9fl oz) full-fat crème fraîche
salt and freshly ground black pepper

An 'authentic' *gratin dauphinois* contains neither egg nor cheese but only potatoes, milk and crème fraîche. The Savoyard gratin, on the other hand, is always made with Beaufort cheese and often with bacon lardons but without either cream or egg. For the Savoyard version, the potatoes are cooked in stock.

1. Cut the potatoes into thin rounds.
2. Preheat the oven to 220°C (425°F), Gas Mark 7. Rub the garlic cloves over the base and sides of a gratin dish, then grease the dish generously with half the butter.
3. Layer up the potato slices evenly in the dish, sprinkling each layer with grated Emmental and seasoning with a little salt, pepper and nutmeg.
4. Bring the milk and crème fraîche to the boil in a saucepan and add a little salt.
5. Pour the milk and crème fraîche over the potatoes and then dot with small pieces of the remaining butter. Bake for 50 minutes until the top is golden brown. Serve immediately.

Spätzle with Brown Butter

SPÄTZLES AU BEURRE NOISETTE

Serves 6 | **Preparation time: 15 mins** | **Resting time: 1 hour** | **Cooking time: 15 mins**

Ingredients

4 large eggs (or 5 small)
pinch of salt
pinch of freshly grated nutmeg
250g (9oz) plain flour
1 tablespoon semolina
1 tablespoon oil
60g (2¼oz) butter

Spätzle are a type of ribbon-shaped egg noodle that are popular in Alsace and parts of central and south-eastern Europe where they are generally served as an accompaniment to stews or other meat dishes with a sauce. The dough is pushed through the holes of a special spätzle maker, or simply a large-holded metal strainer, placed over a saucepan of boiling water so that the ribbons drop directly into the water and cook.

1 Beat the eggs in a mixing bowl with the salt, nutmeg and 50ml (2fl oz) cold water. Gradually mix in the flour and semolina, a little at a time, until you have a smooth and quite soft dough. Wrap the dough in greaseproof paper and let it rest for a minimum of 1 hour in the refrigerator.

2 Bring 5 litres (8¾ pints) salted water and the oil to the boil in a large pan. Place a large-holed metal strainer over the top, add the dough to the strainer and press it lightly with a wooden spoon so that the dough drops through the holes in ribbons into the boiling water. Work in batches to avoid overcrowding the pan.

3 The spätzle are cooked when they rise to the surface of the water. Lift them out with a slotted spoon or skimmer, drain them on kitchen paper and transfer them to a hot plate.

4 Meanwhile, melt the butter in a large frying pan, and when it begins to colour and has a nutty smell, add the spätzle. Toss them in the butter and serve immediately.

Apple Strudel

STRUDEL AUX POMMES

Serves 8–10

Preparation time: 50 mins

Resting time: 2 hours

Cooking time: 40 mins

Ingredients

For the pastry

300g (10½oz) plain flour, plus extra for dusting

1 teaspoon salt

1 egg yolk

2–3 tablespoons oil

For the filling

700g (1lb 9oz) apples (see recipe introduction)

160g (5¾oz) butter, melted, plus extra for greasing

150g (5½oz) soft light brown sugar

150g (5½oz) raisins

40g (1½oz) dried breadcrumbs

100g (3½oz) walnut halves, toasted and chopped

1 teaspoon ground cinnamon

icing sugar, for dusting

Originally a Viennese speciality, apple strudel's popularity soon spread to many parts of Europe, including Alsace, where it is delicious served warm or cold with vanilla ice cream, custard or whipped cream. When making the filling, it is important to use a variety of apple that does not disintegrate when cooked, such as Cox, Granny Smith or Braeburn.

1 First make the pastry. Sift the flour into a mixing bowl and make a well in the centre. In a small bowl, whisk together the salt, egg yolk and oil with 200ml (7fl oz) warm water, pour into the well and rapidly mix the ingredients together to make a soft dough. Shape the dough into a ball, transfer it to a lightly floured work surface and knead until the dough is smooth and elastic. Wrap it in greaseproof paper and leave to rest for 2 hours in the refrigerator.

2 Meanwhile, prepare the filling. Peel the apples, remove their pips and cores and cut into small dice. Heat 100g (3½oz) of the melted butter in a frying pan over a medium heat and cook the apples until they are golden. Stir in the rest of the filling ingredients, apart from the remaining butter, remove the pan from the heat and leave to cool.

3 Begin by rolling the pastry using a rolling pin on a lightly floured work surface and then lift it on to a large clean tea towel that has been dusted with flour. Slide your hands flat underneath the pastry and, working from the centre towards the edges, begin stretching the pastry with your fingers. Continue doing this gently so as not to tear the pastry until it is so thin you can see your hands through it. Trim the pastry edges neatly with kitchen scissors or a sharp knife and then brush it with half the remaining melted butter.

4 Spread the filling over the pastry, leaving a 3cm (1¼-inch) border all round, then roll up the strudel from one long side, using the tea towel to lift the pastry and help you roll it.

5 Preheat the oven to 190°C (375°F), Gas Mark 5. Grease a baking sheet with butter and carefully lift the strudel on to it, curling both ends inwards if it is very long, making sure the join is underneath. Brush with the remaining melted butter and bake for about 35 minutes until golden brown. Serve dusted with icing sugar.

The Bountiful Loire

The historically fruit-producing regions of Anjou and Maine still lead national French fruit production, with orchards extending over 9,000 hectares (22,240 acres). Among the region's leading varieties are pome fruits (with seeds) including several types of apples from Granny Smith to Reine des Reinettes and Jonagold. The pear is also a fruit that is native to these lands, with varieties such as the meltingly soft Comice, the juicy Williams or the sweet Conference.

THE FINEST
ORCHARD FRUITS

Roussillon's Red-freckled Apricot

This is instantly recognizable in summer markets due to its red colour and small spots that dot its skin. For a long time, Roussillon's red-freckled apricot was shunned by consumers because of its spots, despite the fact that it is one of the most fragrant and delicious varieties of apricot there is. As with peaches, apricots originally grew in vineyards, but today the trees are grown in orchards and the red apricot of Roussillon accounts for half the region's production. Eaten fresh in July and August, it can also be bottled or turned into juices and liqueurs – plenty to ensure 'apricot frenzy' lasts all year.

Limousin's Golden Apple

Since ancient times, the Limousin region has been at the heart of apple-growing in France, but the Limousin apple really came into its own in 1950 with the arrival of Golden Delicious. Crunchy and juicy, its flesh is an attractive pinkish colour, due to sunny days alternating with cold nights on the Limousin plateaux and part of the Dordogne where the apple grows. In 2005, it became the only French apple to be awarded AOC status. All are good reasons for you to give into temptation and bite into it!

Guadeloupe's Bottle Pineapple

This variety of pineapple, grown exclusively in Guadeloupe, does not get its name because it is perfect for preparing a good infused rum but instead from its characteristic elongated shape. In the local shops and markets it is also known as *z'annana* or sugar loaf, and it remains green even when it is ripe. Grown north of the capital, Basse-Terre, it is very sweet and is traditionally eaten fresh, on its own or served in wine.

Plougastel's Beautiful Strawberries

In the 18th century when wild strawberries were already known, the explorer Amédée-François Frézier (a name determined by fate, as *fraise* is French for 'strawberry') imported strawberry plants from Chile and settled in Brest, a port-city in Brittany. The Plougastel region of Finistère gradually concentrated on growing this fragile fruit, reaching its peak around 1950. Although there is no variety of strawberry that is specific to Plougastel-Daoulas, several different varieties are grown there, including the famous *gariguette*, which is picked from April onwards.

Kougelhopf

KOUGLOF

Serves 6

Preparation time: 45 mins

Resting time: 1½ hours

Cooking time: 45 mins

Ingredients

100g (3½oz) raisins

2 tablespoons kirsch

20g (¾oz) fresh yeast (or 7g/¼oz sachet fast-action dried yeast)

200ml (7fl oz) warm milk

500g (1lb 2oz) plain flour

2 eggs, beaten

100g (3½oz) sugar

large pinch of salt

150g (5½oz) butter, diced and softened, plus extra for greasing

about 20 whole unblanched almonds

icing sugar, for dusting

This traditional Alsatian brioche can be served at any time of day, whether at breakfast, with morning coffee or afternoon tea, or even with a pre-dinner aperitif.

1 Soak the raisins in the kirsch in a small bowl. If using fresh yeast, crumble it into half the warm milk in a bowl, add 50g (1¾oz) of the flour and mix well. If using dried yeast, stir it into 50g (1¾oz) of the flour in a bowl, add half the warm milk and mix well. Cover the bowl with a clean tea towel and leave in a warm place for about 30 minutes until the dough doubles in volume.

2 Sift the rest of the flour into a large mixing bowl. Make a well in the centre and add the yeast mixture, beaten eggs, the remaining milk, the sugar and salt. Mix everything together and then knead the dough for about 15 minutes. Gradually incorporate the butter and continue kneading until the dough no longer sticks to your fingers. Finally, add the raisins and any kirsch remaining in the bowl and mix well. Put the dough in a clean bowl, cover with the tea towel and leave to rest for 1 hour.

3 Preheat the oven to 180°C (350°F), Gas Mark 4. Thoroughly grease a large 22cm (8½-inch) *kouglof* or bundt tin with butter and sit a whole almond in each of the indentations around the base. Briefly knead the dough again and press it into the tin until it almost fills it. Bake for about 45 minutes, covering with a sheet of foil if the top starts to brown too much. Leave to cool on a wire rack before turning the kugelhopf out and dusting it generously with icing sugar.

Madeleines

Makes 24

Preparation time: 20 mins

Chilling time: 30 mins

Cooking time: 8–10 mins

Ingredients

120g (4¼oz) butter, plus extra for greasing

3 eggs

130g (4½oz) sugar

pinch of salt

150g (5½oz) plain flour, plus extra for dusting

1 teaspoon baking powder

These pretty little shell-shaped sponge cakes come from the towns of Commercy and Liverdun in Lorraine. There are many stories as to how they got their name, from a pilgrim named Madeleine bringing the recipe back from Compostela, to Louis XV being so delighted with the cakes that he introduced them to the court at Versailles, naming them after another cook, also called Madeleine, who had baked them for him.

1 Melt the butter and leave it to cool until lukewarm. Crack the eggs into a mixing bowl and whisk them with the sugar and salt until the mixture is pale and mousse-like.

2 Sift in the flour and baking powder and fold in lightly together with the melted butter. When the mixture is smooth and evenly combined, chill it for 30 minutes in the refrigerator.

3 Preheat the oven to 220°C (425°F), Gas Mark 7. Grease two 12-hole madeleine tins with butter and dust with flour. Spoon in the mixture, filling the holes by two-thirds. Bake for 8–10 minutes, checking the colour of the madeleines regularly. They are cooked when the rounded tops are golden brown. Turn out and leave to cool on a wire rack.

The Mediterranean Rim

Aïoli with all the Trimmings

LE GRAND AÏOLI

Serves 6

Preparation time: 1 hour

Soaking time: 24 hours

Cooking time: 30–40 mins

Ingredients

6 dried salt cod fillets, weighing 150g (5½oz) each

3 large artichokes (or 6 Petit Violet (*poivrade*) artichokes – see page 282)

6 medium waxy potatoes, washed but unpeeled

2 bunches of small, thin carrots, trimmed

2 bunches of baby turnips with long green tops

1 medium cauliflower, stalk removed and divided into small florets

a handful of green beans, trimmed (optional)

500g (1lb 2oz) mussels

50ml (2fl oz) dry white wine

1 shallot, sliced

2 cooked beetroot, cut into wedges and reheated for serving

6 hard-boiled eggs

salt and freshly ground black pepper

For the aïoli

10–12 garlic cloves, peeled

3–4 pinches of salt

3 egg yolks

750ml (1⅓ pints) olive oil

Aïoli is popular throughout Provence. Serve this creamy, garlicky sauce with a selection of vegetables to accompany pre-dinner drinks or turn it into a more substantial dish by adding fish, shellfish and hard-boiled eggs.

1. The day before, put the salt cod fillets in a large bowl of cold water and leave to soak for 24 hours to remove the excess salt, changing the water 2 or 3 times.

2. The next day, cut or snap off the stalks of large artichokes (no need if using small ones). Cook the vegetables separately in pans of boiling water: 20–30 minutes for large artichokes (15 minutes for small ones), 20 minutes for the potatoes, 10–15 minutes for the carrots and turnips, 5–10 minutes for the cauliflower florets and beans (if using).

3. To prepare the mussels, pull away the thread-like 'beards' attached to the shells and scrape the shells under cold water with a small knife to remove any barnacles. Avoid soaking the mussels in cold water, as this will make them open. If any have opened, tap the shells gently and they should close again. If not, discard them, along with any mussels that have cracked or broken shells. Set aside in the refrigerator if not cooking them immediately.

4. Prepare the aïoli. Put the garlic cloves in a large mortar and, using a pestle, crush them with the salt. Add the egg yolks and work them into the crushed garlic for about 2 minutes. Leave to stand for 5 minutes. Add the oil, drop by drop to begin with, then in a thin stream, stirring continuously in the same direction with a wooden spoon. Once the aioli is emulsified and very firm, season with pepper.

5. Heat a pan of water until simmering but not boiling. Drain the salt cod fillets, add to the pan and cook them for 3–4 minutes with the water still simmering. Drain well and transfer them to a serving platter. Put the mussels in a large, lidded pan, add the wine and shallot. Cover the pan and cook over a high heat for 5–8 minutes until all the shells have opened, shaking the pan from time to time. Drain, discarding the cooking juices and any mussels that remain tightly closed.

6. Drain all the vegetables as they cook and add to the serving platter with the reheated beetroot. Cut large artichokes into wedges or small ones in half lengthways. Shell and halve the hard-boiled eggs. Add to the platter with the mussels. Serve the aïoli in a separate bowl.

Salade Niçoise

Serves 4–6

Preparation time: 40 mins

Cooking time: 10 mins

Ingredients

5 eggs

1 small lettuce

1 bunch of spring onions

12–18 salted anchovy fillets

1 lemon

3 or 4 purple Petits Violets artichoke hearts in oil, drained

2 tablespoons white wine vinegar

5 tablespoons olive oil

6–8 tomatoes, quartered

1 red pepper, cored, deseeded and sliced into thin strips

2 × 200g (7oz) cans tuna in olive oil (or spring water), drained and flaked

3 celery sticks, cut into small dice

100g (3½oz) small black Niçoise olives, pitted

salt and freshly ground black pepper

Originating in the Mediterranean city of Nice, this salad makes excellent use of the locally caught tuna and anchovies, mixing them with tomatoes, hard-boiled eggs and small Niçoise black olives for a colourful and satisfying lunch dish to be enjoyed outside with a glass of chilled Provençal rosé when the weather is hot.

1 Hard-boil the eggs in a saucepan of boiling water for 10 minutes.

2 Meanwhile, wash the lettuce, separate it into leaves and pat them dry with kitchen paper. Remove any discoloured outer layers from the spring onions and trim and discard the tops, then slice the green parts.

3 Rinse the anchovies under cold running water to remove the excess salt. Squeeze the juice from the lemon over the artichoke hearts and then cut them into strips. Drain and cool the hard-boiled eggs under cold water. Shell and cut them in half.

4 Prepare a vinaigrette. Whisk together the vinegar and oil, and season with salt and pepper.

5 Line a large shallow serving dish with a few lettuce leaves and then add some of the tomatoes, artichoke slices, red pepper strips, tuna flakes, white spring onion parts, diced celery and sliced green spring onion parts. Continue these layers until all the ingredients have been used up.

6 Pour the vinaigrette over the salad and toss the ingredients gently together. Arrange the hard-boiled egg halves and the anchovies on top and finish with the olives.

Pissaladière

Serves 4–6

Preparation time: 15 mins

Resting time: 1 hour

Cooking time: 45 mins

Ingredients

500g (1lb 2oz) pizza dough or bread dough (bought or homemade)

plain flour, for dusting

120ml (4¼fl oz) olive oil

1kg (2lb 4oz) onions, sliced

3 garlic cloves, crushed

1 thyme sprig

½ bay leaf

1 tablespoon capers

25 salted anchovy fillets

20 small black Niçoise olives, pitted

salt and freshly ground black pepper

In the area around Nice the anchovy is the king of fish, and in this Provençal version of an Italian pizza, anchovies provide a savoury contrast to the sweet onions. Anchovies are also used to make *pissalat*, a condiment of puréed fish marinated in salt and herbs that is used in many local dishes.

1 Put the dough on a lightly floured work surface and lightly flatten it. Drizzle over 4 tablespoons of the oil and then knead it with your hands to incorporate the oil into the dough. Gather the dough into a ball, place in a bowl and cover with a clean tea towel, then leave it to rise at room temperature for 1 hour.

2 Heat the remaining oil in a large frying pan and add the onions, a small pinch of salt, a little pepper, the garlic, thyme, bay leaf and capers. Cover the pan and cook over a low heat for about 25 minutes or until the onions are meltingly soft.

3 Preheat the oven to 240°C (475°F), Gas Mark 9. Flatten the dough into a circle about 1.5cm (⅝ inch) thick. Line a baking sheet with nonstick baking paper and lift the dough circle on to it. Spread the onions over the dough, without going right to the edges.

4 Rinse the anchovies under cold running water to remove the excess salt, then pat them dry with kitchen paper and arrange them over the onions in a lattice pattern. Add the olives, pressing them down lightly.

5 Lift and fold over the edge of the dough a little to form a border to keep the topping in place while in the oven. Bake for 20 minutes and serve warm or cold.

Bastia-style Storzapreti

STORZAPRETI À LA BASTIA

Serves 4

Preparation time: 30 mins

Cooking time: 20 mins

Ingredients

1kg (2lb 4oz) fresh spinach (or 3 bunches of chard or 400g/14oz spinach and 2 bunches of chard)

3 eggs

400g (14oz) fresh Corsican Brocciu cheese – see page 129 (or use ricotta)

chopped fresh mixed herbs (a few sprigs of each type), such as parsley, chervil, marjoram and mint, plus extra sprigs to garnish

plain flour, for coating and dusting

2 tablespoons olive oil

200ml (7fl oz) passata

100g (3½oz) hard cheese such as Gruyère or Emmental, grated

30g (1oz) butter, cut into small pieces

salt and freshly ground black pepper

These baked cheese and vegetable dumplings are a speciality of Bastia, one of the main ports on Corsica, and in the local dialect *storzapreti* means 'priest choker'. The name is not to be confused with *strozzapreti* is a long, rolled pasta that is popular in northern and central Italy.

1 If you are using chard, separate the white stalks and green leaves. Keep the stalks for another recipe. Bring a large saucepan of salted water to the boil, add the spinach or chard (or both, if using), and once the water has returned to the boil, cook for 1 minute. Drain and cool the leaves under cold running water, then squeeze them thoroughly between your hands to extract the maximum amount of water. Chop the leaves as finely as possible. Beat the eggs in a bowl with salt and pepper to season.

2 Put the Brocciu in a mixing bowl and mash it thoroughly with a fork. Add the chopped leaves, herbs and beaten eggs. Mix well then taste and adjust the seasoning, if necessary.

3 Bring a second large saucepan of water to the boil. Spread out some flour on a plate and dust your hands with more flour. Using your hands, shape the mixture into balls the size of a small mandarin and roll them in flour until coated. Add several balls, one at a time, to the boiling water, making sure they are not touching. When the balls rise to the surface, lift them out with a slotted spoon or skimmer and leave them to drain on kitchen paper. Cook all the balls in the same way.

4 Preheat the oven grill. Brush a large, shallow flameproof dish with the oil and arrange the *storzapreti* in it in a single layer. Coat them with the passata and sprinkle over the grated cheese. Dot with the small pieces of butter and grill for about 10 minutes until the *storzapreti* are golden brown on top. Serve immediately, garnished with herb sprigs.

Provençal Veal Shank

JARRET DE VEAU À LA PROVENÇALE

Serves 4–6

Preparation time: 15 mins

Cooking time: 1 hour 40 mins

Ingredients

4 or 6 veal shank slices on the bone, weighing about 180g (6¼oz) each

6 or 8 tomatoes

3 tablespoons olive oil

2 onions, sliced

200ml (7fl oz) dry white wine

1 bouquet garni

150ml (5fl oz) veal stock

2 garlic cloves, crushed

salt and freshly ground black pepper

Slices of veal shank are the cut of meat used for making an Italian *osso buco* and the delicately flavoured, tender meat works equally well in this Provençal version of the dish.

1. Season the slices of veal shank with salt and pepper. Plunge the tomatoes into a saucepan of boiling water for 1 minute. Drain and cool them in a bowl of cold water, then drain again and peel off the skins. Remove the seeds and chop the tomatoes into pieces.

2. Heat the oil in a large sauté pan over a medium-high heat and brown the veal shank slices on each side.

3. Lower the heat, add the onions and fry until lightly golden. Add the wine and bouquet garni. Stir well and cook for 5 minutes.

4. Pour in the stock and add the garlic. Cover the pan and cook over a low heat for 1 hour and 20 minutes, uncovering for the last 10 minutes so that the sauce can reduce. Serve immediately.

Avignon Beef Daube

DAUBE D'AVIGNON

Serves 6–8

Preparation time: 30 mins

Marinating time: 12 hours

Cooking time: 2 hours 10 mins

Ingredients

2kg (4lb 8oz) boneless lamb shoulder

4 carrots

3 onions, chopped

1 thyme sprig

1 bay leaf

2 sage leaves, chopped, plus extra to garnish

2 parsley sprigs, chopped

strip of orange zest, about 5cm (2in) long

100ml (3½fl oz) olive oil

500ml (18fl oz) dry white wine

200g (7og) salt pork belly (or use unsmoked streaky bacon)

2 garlic cloves, crushed

salt and freshly ground black pepper

Also known as a *daube du Comta*, this recipe is very typical of Provençal cuisine. In days gone by it was only served at special family celebrations. The authentic French recipe uses *petit-salé* or salt pork belly, but since this may be difficult to buy outside of France, unsmoked streaky bacon makes an acceptable alternative.

1 The day before, cut the lamb shoulder into large pieces, about 100g (3½oz) each. Trim the carrots and cut lengthways in half.

2 Put the pieces of lamb, carrots, onions, thyme, bay leaf, chopped herbs and orange zest in a large bowl. Season with salt and pepper. Add about three-quarters of the oil and turn all the ingredients over with your hands so that they are coated. Pour in the wine and mix again. Cover the bowl with clingfilm and leave to marinate overnight or for 12 hours in the refrigerator.

3 The next day, lift the meat out of the marinade, reserving the marinade, and place it on a plate lined with kitchen paper. Blot the meat thoroughly with more kitchen paper.

4 Cut the salt pork belly (or bacon) into lardons. Heat the remaining oil in a large frying pan and fry the lardons over a medium heat until they are golden. Add the pieces of lamb and brown them lightly as well, turning them over several times. Drain the lamb and lardons from the pan and transfer them to a flameproof casserole.

5 Pour the reserved marinade and vegetables into the casserole, add the garlic and season with a little salt. Cover the casserole and cook over a very low heat for 2 hours. Remove the thyme sprig, bay leaf and the orange zest before serving, garnished with a little extra chopped sage sprinkled over.

Camargue Bull Stew

GARDIANE DE TAUREAU

Serves 4

Preparation time: 10 mins

Marinating time: 24 hours

Cooking time: 3 hours

Ingredients

1kg (2lb 4oz) braising steak (preferably bull meat from the Camargue)

1 litre (1¾ pints) red wine (preferably Costières de Nîmes)

5 tablespoons red wine vinegar (optional)

1 thyme sprig, chopped

1 rosemary sprig, chopped

pinch of coarse sea salt

pinch of freshly ground black pepper

2 onions, each stuck with 1 clove

2 tablespoons plain flour

2 tablespoons olive oil

flat leaf parsley sprigs, to garnish

Gardiane de taureau **is the traditional dish of the Camargue, an area of lakes and marshland between the Mediterranean and the two arms of the Rhône delta. The stew is named after the guardians of the black bulls that are raised there and are able to roam semi-free. The bulls graze on the natural vegetation, which helps preserve the local ecosystem and gives their meat a distinctive and delicious flavour.**

1. The day before, cut the beef into pieces, weighing 60–80g (2¼–3oz) each. Pour the wine and vinegar (if using) into a large bowl. Add the thyme and rosemary with the salt, pepper and onions stuck with cloves. Mix well and then add the pieces of meat. Cover the bowl with clingfilm and leave to marinate for 24 hours in the refrigerator.

2. The next day, drain the meat, blot it dry with kitchen paper and dust the pieces lightly with the flour. Strain the marinade and coarsely chop the onions.

3. Heat the oil in a flameproof casserole over a medium heat and fry the pieces of beef and onions for about 10 minutes, turning them regularly. Add the marinade and mix well, then cook gently, uncovered, for 45 minutes. Cover the casserole and leave to cook over a low heat for 2 hours.

4. Drain the meat from the casserole and pass the sauce through a fine-mesh sieve, pressing down on the onion pulp to extract all its flavour. Serve the meat with the strained cooking juices, garnished with parsley sprigs, and accompany with red Camargue rice.

Pan-fried Vegetables with Petit Violet Artichokes

BROUILLADE DE PETITS VIOLETS

Serves 6

Preparation time: 20 mins

Cooking time: 55 mins

Ingredients

30 Petit Violet (*poivrade*) artichokes
juice of 1 lemon
4 green tomatoes, such as 'Green zebra'
2 ripe red tomatoes
200g (7oz) back bacon, cut into lardons
2 garlic cloves, finely chopped
2 small white onions, finely chopped
5 tablespoons olive oil
1 thyme sprig
2 bay leaves
10 basil leaves, plus extra to garnish

Petits Violets (also known locally as *poivrades*) are small, purple artichokes that are native to Provence and feature in many of the region's traditional dishes. They can be bought individually or in bunches.

1 Snip off the end of each artichoke leaf with kitchen scissors. Cut the artichokes in half lengthways and remove any hairy choke from the centre. Coat all sides of the leaves with the lemon juice.

2 Cut the green and red tomatoes into thick slices or quarters.

3 Brown the lardons in a large frying pan, then remove and drain them on kitchen paper. Add the tomatoes and garlic to the pan and season with salt and pepper. Sauté for 5 minutes and then drain.

4 Add the prepared artichokes and onions to the pan, drizzle the oil over them and stir until browned. Pull the leaves off the thyme sprig, scatter them over the artichokes and onions and add the bay leaves. Cook for 10 minutes and then return the tomatoes, garlic and lardons to the pan. Cover and leave to simmer for 20 minutes.

5 Roughly chop the basil leaves and add them to the pan. Leave to cook for another 10 minutes and then serve garnished with extra basil leaves.

Tip

These pan-fried vegetables can accompany grilled lamb chops, veal escalopes or tournedos. They can also be eaten cold as a starter, dressed with an olive oil vinaigrette with lemon juice, a little garlic and tarragon.

VEGETABLES
GALORE!

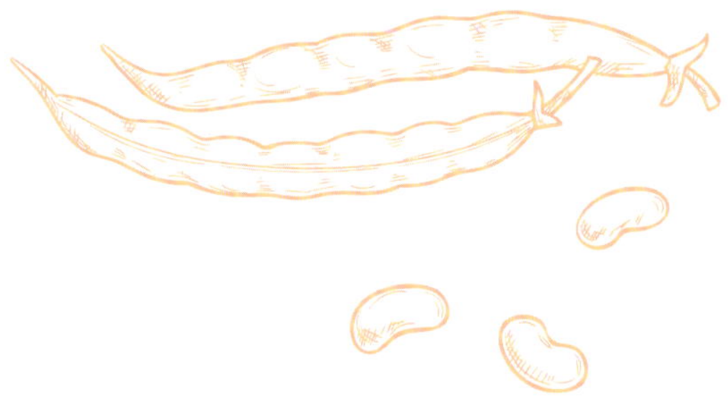

Sand Carrots Come out Tops

As their name tells us, sand carrots have the distinction of growing in sandy soil, which gives them a crunchier texture and sweeter flavour. This has earned them AOC certification and the award of a Label Rouge. Grown in Cotentin, also known as the Cherbourg Peninsula, the carrots can be found on many market stalls in France and are easy to recognize by the fine layer of sand covering them. This is simply removed by brushing the carrots under cold running water, but take care to clean them thoroughly before eating or it might not just be a carrot your teeth are crunching on!

No Has-bean!

The Coco de Paimpol bean first appeared during the 1930s in Brittany, where broad beans, peas and other beans for drying had long been cultivated. History recounts that a sailor called Claude le Diaoul, but nicknamed Claude 'le coco' because of his political leanings (*coco* is French slang for a communist), brought some of the beans back from a trip to Argentina and gave them his nickname. Since then, cultivation of the Coco de Paimpol bean has expanded and many Breton farmers now grow it, following the specifications imposed by its AOC. Although modern technology is used to cultivate it, growing the bean has not given in to the demands of capitalism and industrialization, since much of the harvesting is still done by hand.

Precious Little Truffles

Périgord's black truffle (*Tuber melanosporum*) grows underground, developing close to the root system of its host tree, most frequently an oak. Harvesting the truffles is still done using an animal sensitive to its aroma, usually a trained dog and rarely a pig, contrary to common belief. In Périgord, as well as Quercy, this 'black diamond' has elevated French cuisine and been the inspiration for many recipes, from the simplest – an omelette or scrambled eggs with the truffles – to the most luxurious, such as truffled foie gras.

A Super Tuber!

The most important produce grown on the Île de Noirmoutier in the Bay of Biscay between 1920 and 1960, the Bonnotte potato almost did not survive the arrival of mechanized harvesting, as it would have caused too much damage to plants that were already very fragile. This potato therefore became much sought after, which raised both its profile and its price. Today, production of it has recovered, thanks to the Rennes and Nantes agricultural research laboratories that have been able to strengthen the tuber and revive cultivation. Its yellow, firm-textured flesh makes it the potato of choice, prized by many leading chefs and served at the best restaurants.

Courgettes and Chard are just so Nice

Whenever Nice is mentioned, enjoying a well-filled *pain bagnat* or a slice of beautifully soft *pissaladière* (see recipe page 272) on the Promenade des Anglais immediately springs to mind, but the Niçoise region also produces excellent vegetables, notably courgettes and chard, which are used in many mouth-watering recipes such as stuffed courgettes and chard tart. Courgette flowers are also filled with a stuffing and deep-fried in batter like fritters. There are three different varieties of Nice courgettes: half-length, round and long, the latter being cylindrical and not grooved. Chard, known in Nice as *bette* or *poirée*, is similar to spinach but its leaves and ribs are thicker.

Eul'chicon! (Yuck, chicory!)

Chicory, also known as endive, is a popular vegetable in northern France. It is grown from chicory roots that are kept in darkness to force the production of crisp, white leaves. Often eaten raw in salads, it can also be cooked in different ways, such as grilled, braised or as a gratin. It is used in numerous regional dishes, including the famous tart *flamiche aux chicons*, made with chicory, bacon and crème fraîche. Unfortunately for the poor *chicon*, it is often associated with terrible memories of canteen food, which often denies it the respect it deserves in the collective gustatory imagination!

A FEW OF FRANCE'S
BEST VEGETARIAN RECIPES

MADE WITH ONLY THE FINEST LOCAL PRODUCE

Flemish-style Asparagus

A dish to eat on its own as a starter or serve as an accompaniment to a main course, made with the delicious asparagus coming from the north.

See recipe page 8.

BORDEAUX-STYLE CEPS

All the flavour of these incomparable mushrooms is brought out in this tasty dish from the Gironde region.

See recipe page 106.

COUSINA

A soup flavoured with the finest chestnuts from the Ardèche. Enjoy it with slices of country bread or baguette with butter for a complete meal.

See recipe page 192.

Vegetable Tian

Aubergines, tomatoes, courgettes... all the vegetables of the south come together in this traditional recipe.

See recipe page 288.

REAL COMFORT FOOD

Maroilles Cheese Tart

What dish could be more delicious than a mellow tart filled with melting grilled cheese?

See recipe page 10.

ARDÈCHE CRIQUES

Deliciously crisp potato pancakes to serve as a main meal or as an accompaniment.

See recipe page 204.

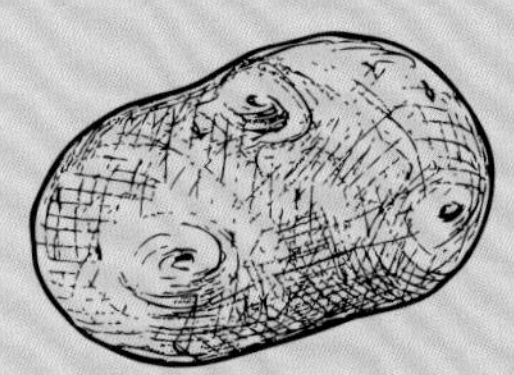

ALIGOT

Not just mashed potatoes, but mashed potatoes with crème fraîche and threads of melting cheese. Irresistible and nostalgic.

See recipe page 218.

TO SPREAD OR TO NIBBLE

GOUGÈRES

Small, cheese-flavoured choux buns to enjoy on their own or to serve with an aperitif. A gourmet indulgence!

See recipe page 122.

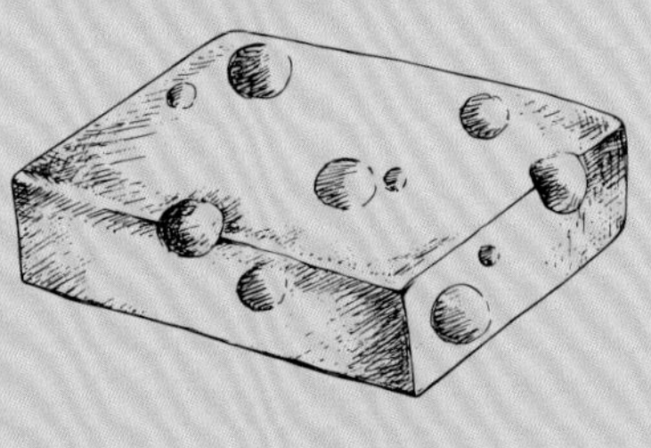

Stir-fried Vegetable Relish

Deliciously crunchy and very aromatic vegetables to make your taste buds tingle.

See recipe page 330.

CANUT'S BRAIN

Soft, fresh cheese perfectly flavoured to spread on toasted bread or serve with raw vegetable sticks for dipping.

See recipe page 196.

Vegetable Tian

TIAN DE LÉGUMES

Serves 4

Preparation time: 15 mins

Cooking time: 1¼ hours

Ingredients

4 courgettes
6 tomatoes
2 aubergines
2 white onions
3 tablespoons olive oil
2 garlic cloves, very finely chopped
leaves from 2 thyme sprigs
1 bay leaf
a few basil leaves, cut into very fine strips
salt and freshly ground black pepper

The word 'tian', as well as being the name of the recipe itself, refers to the earthenware dish used in Provence both to bake and serve the vegetables. Typically a tian is formed as an attractive ring of alternating slices of tomatoes, aubergine, courgette and onions.

1 Preheat the oven to 160°C (325°F), Gas Mark 3. Slice the courgettes, tomatoes, aubergines and onions as evenly as possible.

2 Grease an ovenproof dish with some of the oil. Arrange the vegetable slices close together in the dish, standing them upright and alternating them. Sprinkle over the garlic and thyme leaves and add the bay leaf. Drizzle with the remaining oil and season with salt and pepper.

3 Bake for about 1¼ hours. Discard the bay leaf, scatter over the basil strips and serve directly from the dish as an accompaniment to, for example, lamb cutlets and basmati rice.

Tip

An alternative way to prepare this tian is to sauté the onions, courgettes and aubergines in a little oil before transferring them to the dish. If you want to make the recipe even more special, add a few slices of cooking mozzarella or feta and drizzle olive oil over it just before serving. If possible, choose vegetables that will give similar-sized rounds when sliced.

Pistou Soup

SOUPE AU PISTOU

Serves 4–6

Preparation time: 1 hour

Soaking time: 8 hours (if using dried beans)

Cooking time: 2¾ hours (dried beans) or 1½ hours (fresh or canned beans)

Ingredients

125g (4½oz) mixed dried white haricot beans and red kidney beans (or 400g/14oz shelled fresh beans, if available)

2 large, very ripe tomatoes

50ml (2fl oz) olive oil

1 onion, chopped

white part of 1 leek, trimmed, cleaned and thinly sliced or chopped

5 garlic cloves, chopped

250g (9oz) large green beans (preferably runner beans), stringed, trimmed and cut into small dice

2 small courgettes, diced

1 carrot, diced

4 medium potatoes (preferably maincrop), cut into chunks

2 sage (or basil) leaves

leaves from ½ bunch of parsley

150–200g (5½–7oz) pasta shells (optional)

salt and freshly ground black pepper

For the pistou

5 garlic cloves, chopped

leaves from a large bunch of basil

75g (2¾oz) Parmesan cheese, grated

100ml (3½fl oz) olive oil

Pistou soup is a traditional soup from the south of France made with a selection of vegetables and fresh herbs. It is similar to Italian minestrone and the vegetables are likely to include courgettes, tomatoes and green beans, which are simmered slowly in stock with white haricot beans and small pasta shapes. *Pistou* is a purée made by grinding together basil, garlic, olive oil and a grated hard cheese such as Parmesan using a pestle and mortar. You can substitute 400g (14oz) canned beans, rinsed, for the dried beans to save time.

1 If using dried beans, the day before, soak them in cold water overnight or for at least 8 hours.

2 The next day, drain the beans, put them in a saucepan and cover well with fresh water. Bring to the boil, skimming the foam from the surface. Continue boiling vigorously for 10 minutes, then simmer for about 1 hour until tender but still intact, topping up the water as necessary. Leave to cool, then drain.

3 Plunge the tomatoes into a small saucepan of boiling water for 1 minute. Drain and cool them in a bowl of cold water, then drain again and peel off the skins. Cut them into quarters and remove all the seeds.

4 Bring 2.5 litres (4½ pints) of water to the boil in a large saucepan. Heat the oil in a large flameproof casserole over a medium heat and fry the onion until golden.

5 Add the leek and garlic then the tomatoes to the casserole and leave for 10 minutes to reduce a little. Add all the remaining vegetables, including the cooked dried beans (or fresh or canned beans), and herbs and mix well. Carefully pour in the boiling water, then lower the heat to a gentle simmer and leave to cook for 1 hour. Taste and season with salt and pepper. Lift out the potatoes and crush them roughly with a fork. Stir them back into the casserole to thicken the soup. Add the pasta shells (if using) and continue to cook the soup while you make the pistou.

6 Put the garlic in a mortar. Cut the basil leaves into small pieces with kitchen scissors and add to the mortar. Crush them together with a pestle to make a cream. Add the Parmesan and work this into the mixture with the prongs of a fork. Finally, add the oil, drop by drop to begin with, and then in a thin stream, whisking as for making a mayonnaise.

7 Serve the soup with a spoonful of pistou stirred into each bowl.

Sète Fish Stew

BOURRIDE SÉTOISE

Serves 4–6

Preparation time: 30 mins

Cooking time: 40 mins

Ingredients

1 tomato

200ml (7fl oz) olive oil

white part of 1 leek, trimmed, cleaned and sliced into rounds

2 onions, sliced into rounds

2 carrots, sliced into rounds

3 parsley sprigs, chopped, plus extra to garnish

6 garlic cloves, 2 chopped, 4 peeled but left whole

250ml (9fl oz) dry white wine

1.2–1.5kg (2lb 10oz–3lb 5oz) monkfish tail, skinned and cut into portions – ask your fishmonger to do this

1 egg yolk

salt and freshly ground black pepper

This fish stew is a speciality of Sète, a major fishing port. Monkfish (or *baudroie* as it's called in the Mediterranean region) is the main ingredient here, along with white wine, vegetables, fresh herbs and aïoli.

1 Hull the tomato and cut it into small pieces.

2 Heat 2 tablespoons of the oil in a flameproof casserole over a low heat and fry the leek, onions, carrots and tomato until softened. Add the parsley and chopped garlic. Mix well, then pour in 250ml (9fl oz) of water. Season with salt and pepper and leave to cook for 15 minutes, stirring frequently, then add the wine.

3 Meanwhile, heat another 2 tablespoons of the oil in a frying pan. Season the monkfish pieces with salt and fry them over a low heat for 3–4 minutes on each side. Drain them from the pan and reserve the liquid they have released.

4 Crush the vegetables in the casserole or pass them through a vegetable mill. Return the casserole to the heat and add the fish then the reserved liquid. Lower the heat, cover the pan and simmer for 10–15 minutes.

5 Prepare the aïoli. Crush the remaining garlic cloves with a pinch of salt using a pestle and mortar. Add the egg yolk and mix for about 2 minutes. Leave to stand for 5 minutes. Add the remaining oil, drop by drop to begin with, and then in a thin stream, stirring continuously with a spoon in the same direction as for making mayonnaise. Season lightly with pepper.

6 Drain the pieces of fish, put them in a serving dish and keep warm. Reduce the sauce if it is too runny and adjust the seasoning, if necessary. Remove from the heat and briskly whisk in the aïoli. Spoon the sauce over and around the fish and garnish with a sprinkling of chopped parsley. Serve with new potatoes, simply cooked in boiling water then drained and sliced into thick rounds, or with croutons.

Marseille Bouillabaisse

BOUILLABAISSE DE MARSEILLE

Serves 4–6	Preparation time: 45 mins	Cooking time: 1 hour

Ingredients

2kg (4lb 8oz) mixed fish, such as gurnard, monkfish, conger eel, sea bream, John Dory, hake or scorpion fish, plus 10 small crabs (if available)

2 large onions

3 garlic cloves

150ml (5fl oz) olive oil

white parts of 2 leeks, trimmed, cleaned and chopped

3 celery sticks, chopped

3 tomatoes

1 fennel bulb

1 bouquet garni

2 large pinches of saffron threads

1 baguette, sliced

For the rouille

3 garlic cloves, crushed

pinch of coarse salt

2 pinches of freshly ground white pepper

pinch of saffron threads

2 large pinches of cayenne pepper

2 egg yolks, at room temperature

250ml (9fl oz) olive oil

1 Scale, clean and gut the fish as necessary, removing the heads from the different whole fish, reserving the trimmings. Cut the fish into large pieces. Clean the crabs (if using) with a stiff brush and pull away the feathery gills.

2 Chop 1 onion and 1 garlic clove. Heat 100ml (3½fl oz) of the olive oil in a large saucepan and fry the chopped onion and garlic with the leeks and celery until golden. Season with salt and pepper.

3 Add the fish heads and trimmings. Cover with water, bring to the boil and leave to simmer for 20 minutes. Strain, reserving the cooking juices.

4 Meanwhile, plunge the tomatoes into a saucepan of boiling water for 1 minute. Drain and cool them in a bowl of cold water, then drain again and peel off the skins. Cut the tomatoes into pieces.

Tip

You can add some fine breadcrumbs to your rouille if you want it thicker. You can also use a ready-made rouille sauce if you prefer.

5 Chop the remaining onion, garlic cloves and the fennel bulb.

6 Prepare the rouille. Mix together the garlic, coarse salt, white pepper, saffron, cayenne and egg yolks in a large mortar or bowl. Then drizzle in the oil, a little at a time, whisking vigorously.

7 Fry the vegetables in the remaining oil in the saucepan until browned. Add the reserved cooking juices, the tomatoes, bouquet garni and saffron. Add all the fish (and crabs, if using), except the John Dory and/or hake (if using). Cook over a medium-high heat for 8 minutes. Add the John Dory and/or hake, lower the heat and cook for another 5–6 minutes.

8 Remove the pan from the heat but keep the soup hot. Toast the baguette slices in the oven. Drain the fish from the pan and transfer to a large serving dish. Pour the cooking juices into a soup tureen without straining. Serve the fish with the cooking juices spooned over, accompanied with the rouille and toasted baguette slices.

Nîmes Salt Cod Brandade

BRANDADE DE NÎMES

Serves 4–6

Preparation time: 15 mins

Soaking time: 24 hours

Cooking time: 15–20 mins

Ingredients

1kg (2lb 4oz) dried salt cod fillets

450ml (16fl oz) olive oil

400ml (14fl oz) milk

freshly ground white pepper

This dish is a speciality of Nîmes, an ancient city between the Mediterranean and the hills of the Cévennes. It is made by mashing salt cod with olive oil and milk to make a creamy purée. Its name comes from the Provençal word *brandado,* meaning 'stirred', and the success of the recipe depends on slowly beating in the olive oil and milk until the mixture has the texture of light, fluffy mashed potatoes.

1 The day before, soak the salt cod fillets in a large bowl of cold water for 24 hours to remove the excess salt, changing the water 2 or 3 times.

2 The next day, drain the fillets and put them in a large saucepan or flameproof casserole, cover them with plenty of fresh cold water and bring slowly to the boil. Lower the heat and poach the fish for 8 minutes at a very gentle simmer. Drain, leave until just warm, then remove the skin and bones. Flake the flesh using your fingers. Put the flakes in a saucepan and crush them with a wooden spoon.

3 Heat the oil and the milk in 2 separate saucepans.

4 Place the saucepan containing the salt cod over a very low heat. Add 1 tablespoon of hot oil and 1 tablespoon of hot milk alternately to the salt cod, beating with a wooden spoon after each addition as for making mayonnaise. The mixture will have the consistency of creamy mashed potatoes. Season with white pepper, but no extra salt will be needed. Serve with toasted baguette slices.

Tip

You can flavour the brandade with a little black truffle oil from Uzès, if you wish.

Corsican Baked Cheesecake

FIADONE

Serves 4

Preparation time: 20 mins

Draining time: 3 hours

Cooking time: 40 mins

Ingredients

250g (9oz) fresh Brocciu cheese (or use ricotta)

½ unwaxed lemon or 1 tablespoon brandy (eau-de-vie de marc or a fruit brandy)

3 eggs

100g (3½oz) sugar

pinch of salt

20g (¾oz) butter, melted, for greasing

Corsica's traditional cheesecake is made with local Brocciu soft cheese (see page 129) and flavoured with lemon zest or eau-de-vie. It is baked without a biscuit or pastry crust and served cold.

1 Wrap the Brocciu (or ricotta) in muslin and leave it to drain in a sieve placed over a bowl for 3 hours.

2 Using a vegetable peeler, remove a strip of zest, 7–8cm (2¾–3¼ inches) long, from the lemon (if using) and blanch it in a small saucepan of boiling water for 3 minutes. Drain and chop the zest finely.

3 Separate the eggs. Put the yolks in a mixing bowl, add the sugar and beat until smooth and creamy. Add the drained Brocciu (or ricotta) and the finely chopped lemon zest or brandy and mix in.

4 Preheat the oven to 180°C (350°F), Gas Mark 4. Whisk the egg whites with the salt in a clean mixing bowl until standing in stiff peaks. Stir 1 tablespoon into the cheese mixture to soften it before very lightly folding in the rest until incorporated.

5 Grease a 22cm (8½-inch) round deep flan tin or shallow cake tin with the melted butter and pour in the cheesecake mixture. Level the surface and bake for about 35 minutes or until the tip of a knife inserted into the centre of the cheesecake comes out clean. Leave the cheesecake to cool in the tin before turning it out.

Tip

You can also cook the cheesecake in individual tins if you wish, checking whether they are cooked after about 15 minutes.

Oreillettes

Makes about 36

Preparation time: 30 mins

Chilling time: 12 hours

Cooking time: 20 mins

Ingredients

4 egg yolks

2 tablespoons orange flower water (or the finely grated zest of 1 lemon)

300g (10½oz) plain flour

½ teaspoon salt

80g (3oz) butter, cut into small pieces and softened

50g (1¾oz) sugar

sunflower or groundnut oil, for deep-frying, plus extra for greasing

icing sugar, for dusting

***Merveilles, bugnes, oreillettes*... from Lyon to the Riviera and south-west France, you will find variations of these little fritters that are enjoyed as a dessert at Christmas and are especially popular at Easter (they are also known as Mardi Gras fritters). The thinner and more brittle they are, the better.**

1 The day before, make the dough. Beat the egg yolks with the orange flower water (or lemon zest). Sift the flour on to a work surface, make a well in the centre and add the salt, butter, sugar and egg yolk mixture. Bring the ingredients together with your fingertips and knead, adding just enough water to make a very soft dough that no longer sticks to your fingers. This will take about 10 minutes and can be done in a stand mixer fitted with the dough hook, if you wish.

2 Wrap the dough in greaseproof paper and chill it overnight or for 12 hours in the refrigerator.

3 The next day, roll out the dough on an oiled work surface as thinly as possible using a rolling pin, or feed it through a pasta machine. It must be so thin that it is translucent.

4 Heat enough oil for deep-frying in a large pan until very hot but not smoking to 170–180°C (340–350°F). Using a pizza wheel, cut the dough into regular or random shapes, frying them in batches as you go. Ideally, one person cuts them while another cooks them.

5 Fry the oreillettes 2 or 3 at a time. They should cook in around 12 seconds, becoming golden brown and brittle. Use a skimmer to hold them down in the oil and turn them over halfway through cooking. Immediately they are cooked, drain them on kitchen paper. Serve warm or cold, dusted with icing sugar.

Catalan Crème Brûlée

CRÈME BRÛLÉE CATALAN

Serves 4

Preparation time: 15 mins

Infusing time: 12 hours

Chilling time: 2 hours

Cooking time: 10–15 mins

Ingredients

1 litre (1¾ pints) milk

1 cinnamon stick

grated zest of 1 lemon

1 teaspoon green aniseeds

1 vanilla pod

2 eggs

5 egg yolks

150g (5½oz) sugar

25g (1oz) plain flour

25g (1oz) potato flour

A classic Catalan dessert, which is similar to other versions of crème brûlée but lighter because it is made with milk rather than double cream. It is also cooked on the hob instead of in a bain-marie in the oven and flavoured with lemon zest, aniseeds and cinnamon.

1 The day before, put the milk, cinnamon stick, lemon zest and aniseeds in a saucepan. Split the vanilla pod lengthways in half, scrape the seeds into the milk and add the pod. Heat until the milk comes to the boil and then immediately remove the pan from the hob. Leave to cool and then cover with clingfilm and leave to infuse overnight or for 12 hours in the refrigerator.

2 The next day, crack the whole eggs into a separate saucepan, add the egg yolks and whisk lightly until mixed. Add 3 tablespoons of the sugar and then whisk vigorously until the mixture is pale and mousse-like. Mix in the plain and potato flours.

3 Strain the milk and very gradually add this to the whisked egg mixture, stirring continuously. Place the pan over a gentle heat and cook, again stirring continuously, until the mixture thickens. Let the custard boil for only 1 minute and then take the pan off the heat and whisk again.

4 Pour the custard into individual shallow ramekins or baking dishes. Cool and then chill in the refrigerator for 2 hours or until ready to serve. A fairly thick skin should form on top.

5 Spread the remaining sugar over the surface of the custards in an even layer and caramelize using a kitchen blowtorch or under a hot grill for 2 minutes. Serve as soon as the caramel topping has cooled sufficiently.

Overseas

Réunion Rougaille Sauces

ROUGAILS

Preparation time: 10 mins for each rougaille

Mango Rougaille

- 5 or 6 bird's-eye chillies
- 200ml (7fl oz) oil
- 400g (14oz) ripe mangoes
- 10g (¼oz) coarse salt
- 1 large onion

Lime Rougaille

- 200g (7oz) limes
- 4 or 5 bird's-eye chillies
- 1 large onion
- 10g (¼oz) coarse salt
- 200ml (7fl oz) oil

Tomato Rougaille

- 10g (¼oz) coarse salt
- 5 or 6 bird's-eye chillies
- 2 tomatoes
- finely grated zest of 2 limes
- 1 large onion
- 200ml (7fl oz) oil

Tomato Rougaille

Ingredients

2 tomatoes

1 large onion

5 or 6 red bird's-eye chillies, stalks removed, deseeded and chopped

10g (¼oz) coarse salt

2 limes

200ml (7fl oz) oil

Rougailles are aromatic, spicy sauces used in many Creole dishes on the island of Réunion in the Indian Ocean. Tomato and mango rougailles are the best known. Tomato rougaille is served with various meats and mango more often with fish. They pack a powerful punch and are eaten as accompaniments in small quantities.

1 Hull the tomatoes and cut them into small strips. Finely slice the onion.

2 Using a pestle and mortar, crush the chillies with the salt.

3 Finely grate the lime zests.

4 Mix all the ingredients together with the oil.

Mango Rougaille

Ingredients

400g (14oz) ripe green mangoes

1 large onion

5 or 6 bird's-eye chillies, stalks removed, deseeded and chopped

10g (¼oz) coarse salt

200ml (7fl oz) oil

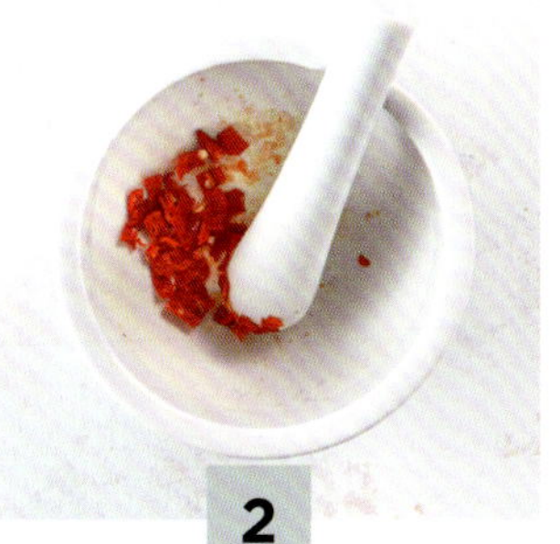

1 Peel the mangoes, cut the flesh away from the stones and chop the flesh into small pieces. Finely slice the onion.

2 Using a pestle and mortar, crush the chillies with the salt.

3 Mix all the ingredients together with the oil.

Lime Rougaille

Ingredients

200g (7oz) lime flesh

1 large onion

4 or 5 bird's-eye chillies, stalks removed, deseeded and chopped

10g (¼oz) coarse salt

200ml (7fl oz) oil

1 Chop the lime flesh into very small dice. Finely slice the onion.

2 Using a pestle and mortar, crush the chillies with the salt.

3 Mix all the ingredients together with the oil.

Salt Cod Fritters

ACRAS DE MORUE

Serves 4

Preparation time: 15 mins

Soaking time: 24 hours

Cooking time: 20 mins

Ingredients

150g (5½oz) dried salt cod

3 spring onions, trimmed

2 garlic cloves, peeled

1 small red chilli, stalk removed and deseeded

½ bunch of parsley

200g (7oz) plain flour

1 teaspoon baking powder

2 eggs, beaten

1 teaspoon dried thyme

oil, for deep-frying

lime wedges, for squeezing over

Salt cod was a European export to the West Indies where today it is a staple of many of the island cuisines and used in a variety of ways: as a fritter called *acra*, as a salad with tomatoes or red peppers called *chiquetaille*, mixed with mashed avocado, finely chopped red onion and chilli in a dip known as *féroce*, or as brandade (see recipe page 298).

1 The day before, soak the salt cod in a large bowl of cold water for 24 hours to remove the excess salt, changing the water 2 or 3 times.

2 The next day, drain the salt cod and put it in a saucepan of fresh cold water. Bring to the boil, then turn off the heat and leave the salt cod to sit in the hot water for 15 minutes. Drain it, leave until just warm, then remove the skin and bones. Flake the flesh into a bowl.

3 Chop the spring onions, garlic, chilli and parsley together using a chopping knife or food processor.

4 Sift the flour and baking powder into a mixing bowl. Add the eggs and mix in a little at a time with 150ml (5fl oz) cold water to make a smooth batter. Add the chopped ingredients, the salt cod flakes and thyme.

5 Heat enough oil for deep-frying to 160–180°C (325–350°F). Add spoonfuls of the mixture to the hot oil, a few at a time, and fry for about 3 minutes until golden brown. Remove the fritters with a slotted spoon or skimmer, drain on kitchen paper and serve hot with lime wedges for squeezing over.

Plantain Banana Stew

DAUBE DE BANANES

Serves 4

Preparation time: 15 mins

Cooking time: 30 mins

Ingredients

6 yellow plantain bananas

juice of 1 lemon

200g (7oz) smoked streaky bacon

6–7 tablespoons oil

6 shallots, chopped

2 garlic cloves, chopped

2 thyme sprigs

piece of red chilli, chopped, plus a few extra slices to garnish

pinch of ground cinnamon

4 flat leaf parsley sprigs, chopped

This popular Creole dish is made with plantains – starchy bananas that are not eaten raw but used as an ingredient in cooked dishes.

1 Peel the plantains and remove all the strings running down them. Cut the plantains into large pieces and toss them with the lemon juice.

2 Chop the bacon into small dice.

3 Heat the oil in a flameproof casserole over a medium heat and fry the bacon until browned, then add the plantains and cook for 3–4 minutes. Add the shallots, garlic, thyme and chilli (you can adjust the amount of chilli according to your personal taste). Mix well and cook for 2–3 minutes.

4 Pour 200ml (7fl oz) of hot water into the casserole, add the cinnamon and mix well. Half-cover the pan and leave to simmer for 15–20 minutes. Sprinkle with the chopped parsley, garnish with a few extra chilli slices and serve.

Tip

As well as this stew, plantains make excellent crisps. Choose unripe plantains, peel and slice them finely and then deep-fry in hot oil at 175°C (345°F) for 5 minutes until golden brown and crisp.

Ouassous with Tomatoes and Chives

OUASSOUS AUX TOMATES ET AUX CIVES

Serves 8

Preparation time: 30 mins

Marinating time: 20 mins

Cooking time: 35 mins

Ingredients

2kg (4lb 8oz) raw ouassous (or other large raw prawns) in their shells

juice of 8 limes

1kg (2lb 4oz) tomatoes

2cm (¾-inch) piece of fresh root ginger

4 tablespoons olive oil

4 onions, sliced

100ml (3½fl oz) aged rum

1 tablespoon tomato purée

1 small red chilli, stalk removed, deseeded and finely chopped, plus a few extra slices to garnish

1 thyme sprig

1 Indian wood leaf (see Tip)

4 garlic cloves, crushed

1 bunch of chives, chopped

10 flat leaf parsley sprigs, very finely chopped

salt and freshly ground black pepper

spring onions, to garnish (optional)

Ouassous are large freshwater prawns that are very popular in Guadeloupe and also Martinique where they are called *z'habitants*. Difficult to find away from the islands, any large raw prawns can be used instead.

1 Rinse and drain the prawns. Put them on a large plate, drizzle the lime juice over them and leave to marinate for 20 minutes, turning them over once or twice.

2 Plunge the tomatoes into a saucepan of boiling water for 1 minute. Drain and cool them in a bowl of cold water, then drain again and peel off the skins. Remove the seeds and crush or finely chop the flesh, then put in a bowl.

3 Scrape the skin off the ginger and slice into thin strips. Heat the oil with the ginger in a large flameproof casserole over a medium heat. Add the onions and fry until they have softened, then add the prawns and fry for 5 minutes. Heat the rum in a small saucepan, pour it into the casserole and flambé (set alight briefly).

4 Dilute the tomato purée by mixing it with 2 tablespoons of cold water. Stir it into the tomatoes along with the chilli, thyme and Indian wood leaf and season with salt and pepper. Add to the casserole, cover and leave to simmer for 20 minutes.

5 Divide the tomato mixture between 8 serving plates, discarding the Indian wood leaf. Top with the prawns and sprinkle with the garlic, chives and parsley. Garnish with a few extra slices of red chilli, and spring onions if you wish, and serve immediately.

Tip

Indian wood leaves come from the West Indian pepper tree, which produces allspice berries. They have a mild flavour, similar to a blend of nutmeg, cinnamon, cloves and pepper. The leaves can be bought online and are used like bay leaves. In this recipe, allspice can be substituted.

Sautéed Swordfish with Lime

TOUFFÉ D'ESPADON AU CITRON VERT

Serves 4

Preparation time: 15 mins

Marinating time: 1 hour

Cooking time: 30 mins

Ingredients

800g (1lb 12oz) swordfish loin or steaks

juice of 4 limes

2 Indian wood leaves – see Tip, page 316 (or bay leaves)

4 garlic cloves, chopped

3 tomatoes

2 tablespoons olive oil

4 onions, sliced

4 shallots, sliced

½ teaspoon *roucou* – annatto food colouring (optional)

fine shreds of lime zest, to garnish

lime wedges, for squeezing over

As in the previous recipe, Indian wood leaves are used to flavour this swordfish dish, but rather than allspice, bay leaves can replace them here. *Roucou* is a West Indian name for annatto, a vivid orange-red food colouring made from the seeds of the roucou or achiote tree.

1 Wash the swordfish and cut it into large pieces. Add half the lime juice to a mixing bowl and crumble in 1 Indian wood leaf (or bay leaf). Add half the garlic to the bowl and then the swordfish pieces. Mix well, cover the bowl with clingfilm and leave to marinate for 1 hour in the refrigerator, turning the pieces of fish over from time to time so that they absorb the flavours of the marinade.

2 Hull the tomatoes and cut them into small pieces. Drain the swordfish from the marinade.

3 Heat the oil in a flameproof casserole over a medium heat and fry the onions and shallots until they are softened and lightly browned. Add the pieces of fish and let them colour a little on all sides. Lastly, add the tomatoes and the remaining garlic and Indian wood leaf (or bay leaf). Cover the casserole, lower the heat and leave to simmer for 15 minutes, stirring regularly.

4 Pour the remaining lime juice into the casserole. Add the *roucou*, stir to mix it in and cook, still over a low heat, for 5 minutes. Serve hot, garnished sprinkled with fine shreds of lime zest, with lime wedges for squeezing over. Accompany with Creole rice, or plain rice flavoured with your favourite spices, if you wish.

A TANGY TWIST
IN THE KITCHEN!

Wild about Corsica's Famous Citrus Fruits!

Corsica is renowned for its stunning scenery, its beaches and mountains, but you may not be aware that it also produces wonderful citrus fruits such as blood oranges, lemons, clementines, pomelos and more. All these fruits are grown in orchards mainly on the island's eastern plain, where the Mediterranean climate is perfectly suited to their cultivation. Corsican citrus fruits are prized for their intense flavour and juiciness, which is largely the result of local producers following traditional growing methods. The fruits are used in many of the island's culinary specialities such as jams, cakes or liqueurs, but they are also highly prized for their extract, which is used in the production of perfumes and beauty products.

Makrut Lime – a Versatile Citrus Fruit

Also known as the Madagascan lime, the makrut lime is a citrus fruit native to Southeast Asia that grows primarily in tropical areas. Shaped like an over-sized lime and with a bumpy surface, it has a very distinctive flavour, combining lemongrass, ginger and coriander. Although there is no (or very little) cultivation of it in mainland France, due to its temperate climate, it can be found in France's overseas departments and territories located in the tropics, such as Guadeloupe, Martinique and Réunion. The last is particularly renowned for its makrut lime production (known as *combava* in Réunion), the fruit being used in many local dishes on the island.

Sweet and Savoury Flavours

Orange juice and lemon juice perfectly complement duck breasts with melt-in-the-mouth caramelized peaches (see recipe page 166).

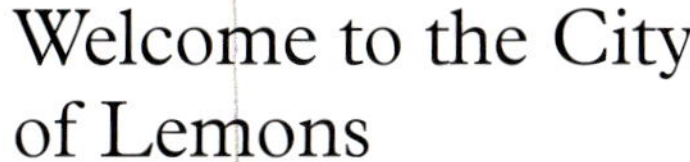

Welcome to the City of Lemons

Regarded as one of the highlights of traditional French Riviera cuisine, the Menton lemon is notable for its stronger aromas and milder, sweeter flavour than ordinary lemons. For centuries this citrus fruit has been grown in Menton, hence the town's nickname of City of Lemons, and a Lemon Festival (Fête du Citron®) is held there every year at the end of winter. Numerous floats decorated with the citrus fruits parade through the streets, celebrating the cultivation of lemon trees in the region. Although it does not yet benefit from AOP or AOC certification, the Menton lemon was awarded the European IGP label in 2015 that guarantees its traceability on the stalls that sell it and therefore its authenticity.

Ones to Try!

For a fragrant, tangy dish, try Sautéed Swordfish with Lime (see recipe page 318) or the Réunion Rougaille Sauces (see recipes pages 308–11).

Rum-baked Gammon

JAMBON AU RHUM

Serves 6

Preparation time: 20 mins

Marinating time: 24 hours

Cooking time: 3 hours

Ingredients

2kg (4lb 8oz) unsmoked boneless gammon joint, rind removed

1 garlic clove, crushed

1 onion, sliced into rounds

6 cloves

2cm (¾-inch) cinnamon stick

1 tablespoon vinegar of choice

2 tablespoons wholegrain mustard

400ml (14oz) white rum

1 pineapple, peeled, cored and cut into chunks

If buying the gammon joint from a butcher, you could ask them to remove the rind and score the surface as instructed in step 1, before rolling and tying with string so that it keeps its shape during cooking. If you get either a fresh or a dry-cured joint, it will not need soaking before cooking. However, taste the meat before serving to check if it needs seasoning with salt, although it probably will not need any.

1 The day before, score the layer of fat over the surface of the gammon in a lattice pattern with a sharp knife. Lift the joint into a large dish.

2 Mix together the garlic, onion, cloves, cinnamon stick, vinegar, mustard and rum, then pour the marinade over the gammon. Cover and leave to marinate for 24 hours in the refrigerator, turning the gammon over frequently and brushing it regularly with the marinade.

3 The next day, preheat the oven to 170°C (325°F), Gas Mark 3. Lift the gammon out of the marinade and pat it dry with kitchen paper. Remove the cinnamon stick from the marinade. Transfer the gammon to a roasting tin, pour over the marinade and cook it in the oven for 2 hours, basting it frequently with the marinade and adding a little water to the tin if the marinade evaporates.

4 Arrange the chunks of pineapple around the gammon and return to the oven for another 1 hour until the meat is cooked through. Remove the gammon from the oven, cover the joint loosely with foil and leave to rest in a warm place for 15 minutes before carving it into slices. Deglaze the roasting tin with water, stirring with a spoon to incorporate the cooking juices sticking to the bottom of it. Pour the juices into a gravy boat, arrange the pineapple around the gammon and serve.

Pork Colombo

COLOMBO DE PORC

Serves 6

Preparation time: 20 mins

Marinating time: 30 mins

Cooking time: 55 mins

Ingredients

1.2kg (2lb 10oz) boneless pork loin

1 ripe green mango

2 medium aubergines

3 potatoes

3 tablespoons groundnut oil

2 spring onions, trimmed and finely chopped

3 tablespoons Colombo powder

juice of 1 lemon

salt and freshly ground black pepper

coriander sprigs, to garnish

For the marinade

2 garlic cloves, chopped

1 small red chilli, stalk removed and cut into thin strips

3 tablespoons vinegar of choice

Although the name might sound Sri Lankan, this dish is in fact a West Indian pork curry made with spices that were originally from the Indian subcontinent. Colombo powder *(poudre de Colombo)*, is made from a mix of spices including coriander, cloves, cumin, fenugreek and turmeric, and it gives warm, subtle notes rather than great heat. If you cannot find it, substitute another curry powder of your choice.

1. First prepare the marinade. Mix the garlic and chilli with the vinegar in a shallow dish and season with salt and pepper.
2. Cut the pork into cubes, then add to the marinade, turning them over so that they are well coated. Leave to marinate for 30 minutes.
3. Meanwhile, peel the mango, cut away the flesh from the stone and chop it into pieces. Peel the aubergines and potatoes, rinse them and cut them into cubes.
4. Heat the oil in a flameproof casserole over a medium heat. Drain the pork from the marinade and add it to the casserole with the mango and spring onions. Stir for about 5 minutes until the onions and pork are golden brown.
5. Mix the Colombo powder with a little water until smooth and add it to the casserole. Add the aubergines and potatoes, season with salt and pepper and stir to mix well. Pour in just enough water to cover the ingredients and bring to the boil. Lower the heat, cover the casserole and leave to cook for 50 minutes.
6. About 5 minutes before the end of the cooking time, add the lemon juice. Taste and adjust the seasoning and then spoon the pork Colombo into a serving dish. Serve hot, garnished with coriander sprigs and accompanied with Creole rice.

Réunion Chicken Curry

CARI DE POULET

Serves 4

Preparation time: 15 mins

Cooking time: 55 mins

Ingredients

1 free-range chicken, weighing 1.4kg (about 3lb)

3 tablespoons olive oil

4 onions, finely chopped

6 garlic cloves, crushed

300g (10½oz) plum tomatoes, thinly sliced

1 teaspoon ground turmeric

salt and freshly ground black pepper

This curry is a very popular dish on the island of Réunion. It is usually served with white rice and a tomato rougaille (see recipe page 310).

1. Cut the chicken into 8 pieces.

2. Heat the oil in a flameproof casserole over a medium heat and fry the chicken until the pieces are golden brown, turning them over several times so that they colour evenly. Add the onions and garlic and sauté until golden. Add the tomatoes and turmeric and cook for another 2–3 minutes.

3. Lower the heat and cover the casserole. Leave to simmer over a very low heat for 45 minutes, stirring from time to time. If necessary, add a little water to prevent the curry from sticking to the casserole. Taste and season with salt and pepper, if needed. Serve hot accompanied with rice and a tomato rougaille.

Goat Massalé

MASSALÉ DE CABRI

Serves 4

Preparation time: 15 mins

Cooking time: 1¼ hours

Ingredients

1kg (2lb 4oz) boneless young goat (kid) loin (or use lamb)

3 tomatoes

50ml (2fl oz) oil

2 onions, sliced

3 dried curry leaves (or 2 bay leaves)

5 garlic cloves, crushed

3 red bird's-eye chillies, stalks removed, deseeded and finely sliced

20g (¾oz) fresh root ginger, peeled and grated or finely chopped

600g (1lb 5oz) potatoes, peeled and cut into pieces

5 or 6 coriander sprigs, to garnish

salt (if needed)

Cabri **is young goat meat that is lean and full of flavour, but it requires slow stewing or braising to ensure it is tender. While it is becoming more widely available through specialist suppliers as well as ethnic food stores and markets, it can be substituted with lamb if you prefer. A striking way to serve the curry, as on the island of Réunion, is to line serving plates with banana leaves and spoon the curry on to those.**

1 Cut the goat meat (or lamb) into 3–4cm (1¼–1½-inch) pieces. Hull the tomatoes, remove their seeds and cut the flesh into pieces.

2 Heat the oil in a flameproof casserole over a medium heat and brown the pieces of meat all over. Add the onions and curry leaves (or bay leaves) and cook until the onions are golden. Then add the garlic, chillies and ginger.

3 Mix well and add the tomatoes and potatoes. Stir until the potatoes are golden and then pour in 250ml (9fl oz) of water. Cover the casserole and cook over a low heat for about 1 hour, stirring from time to time, and seasoning with a little salt, if necessary.

4 Spoon the massalé into a serving dish, garnish with the coriander and serve hot with rice.

Stir-fried Vegetable Relish

ACHARDS DE LÉGUMES

Serves 6

Preparation time: 20 mins

Cooking time: 5 mins

Ingredients

150g (5½oz) chayotes (custard marrow)

150g (5½oz) carrots

50g (1¾oz) green beans

1cm (½-in) piece of fresh root ginger

2 garlic cloves

3 tablespoons groundnut oil

1 onion, sliced

150g (5½oz) small cauliflower florets

1 small red or green chilli, stalk removed, deseeded and cut into thin strips

1 tablespoon ground turmeric

2 tablespoons distilled white vinegar

This Creole dish is a mix of different vegetables cut into thin strips, stir-fried and made into a relish by pouring vinegar into the pan. You can pre-cook the green beans in a saucepan of simmering salted water for 5 minutes if you prefer them not to be too crunchy. *Chayote*, also known as *christophine* or custard marrow, is a type of squash similar in flavour to courgette. It is a locally grown and very popular ingredient on the island of Réunion, but it is also a favourite of many other cuisines including West Indian, Mexican and Chinese.

1 Peel the chayotes then cut them, the carrots and the green beans into long thin strips roughly the same length. Set aside.

2 Peel the ginger and garlic, then crush them finely using a pestle and mortar or small food processor.

3 Heat the oil in a large frying pan over a high heat and stir-fry the onion, cauliflower florets, ginger and garlic, chilli and turmeric. Keeping the heat under the pan high, add the vegetable strips and stir-fry for 2 minutes or until tender. Take the pan off the heat, stir in the vinegar and serve as an accompaniment to a meat or fish dish.

SPICE
THINGS UP!

The Queen of Vanillas

Bourbon vanilla grows on Réunion (formerly known as the island of Bourbon) where it was introduced from Mexico at the beginning of the 18th century. The island's warm, humid climate, along with its volcanic subsoil, proved to be fertile ground for the flower and its precious pod – vanilla is in fact an edible member of the orchid family. The Bourbon variety reveals an intense array of flavours, thanks to the 200-plus aromatics it contains, which make it the undisputed vanilla queen in your very own castle!

Small but Mighty

Make way for the hottest spice that grows in France's overseas territories: the chilli! Introduced into Europe by Christopher Columbus upon his return from the Americas, today more than 200 varieties of chill are cultivated. It is mainly grown in the French Caribbean islands and Guyana where it is often given poetic and childish names, such as 'chilli *zozio*', 'bird' or 'parrot's tongue'. Do not be fooled by these endearing nicknames, though, as the very hot peppers are tiny flavour bombs that will assault your taste buds if you overindulge.

The Chilli Star

The absolute star of the chilli family is Piment d'Espelette, named after the Basque village of Espelette at the foot of the Pyrenees where it is mainly cultivated. It is renowned for its unique taste, a combination of slightly sweet and fruity, but do not trust its innocent appearance! It can also be very spicy, depending on the way it is prepared, whether fresh and whole, dried on a rope or as a powder. Traditionally, it was always a fixture in Basque kitchens where it was used to enhance the flavour of the region's local specialities such as piperade, Basque chicken or Bayonne ham. However, over recent years it has also carved out a place in modern cuisine and is still going from strength to strength. Grown using traditional methods, it is the only French spice to have been awarded AOC status and it even has its own Brotherhood, which holds an annual celebration (although it has not yet been invited to leave its imprint on Hollywood Boulevard!).

Herbs for All Seasons

Rosemary, oregano, savory, thyme, basil: all these herbs are part of the aromatic seasoning known as herbes de Provence. This little powerhouse of flavour from the *garrigue* (the shrubland vegetation of the dry Mediterranean area) boasts no AOC or IGP certification, but nevertheless, its producers have succeeded in obtaining a Label Rouge for it by following precise rules in order to promote regional production.

A Pinch of Salt

The attraction and fame of *sel de Guérande* lies in the way it is produced and harvested. No machines or chemicals are involved, just nature combined with the age-old know-how of the Breton workers in the Guérande salt marshes, which extend over more than 2,000 hectares (5,000 acres). At high tide, seawater rushes into several ponds, which become increasingly saturated with salt, at which point the sun and wind play their part by causing the salt to crystallize on the surface of the marshes. The salt workers can then collect the *gros sel* (cooking salt) and *fleur de sel* (sea salt flakes) using a *las*, a kind of rake with a long handle.

A Toast to Garlic

Notable for its distinctive flavour, Lautrec pink garlic might not do much for your breath, but your taste buds will love it! Very popular in south-west France, a special weekly garlic market is held in Lautrec, a small village in the Tarn department, where it is produced. Lautrec garlic was the first agricultural product to be granted a Label Rouge in 1966 and since 1996 it has held IGP certification. It is particularly appreciated in *aïgo boulido,* a full-flavoured garlic soup that is typical of the region, but it is equally good crushed using a pestle and mortar and added to sauces, chopped and used in salads or rubbed over slices of toasted bread.

Green Papaya Stew

RAGOÛT DE PAPAYA VERTE

Serves 4–6

Preparation time: 30 mins

Soaking time (if using salt cod): 24 hours

Cooking time: 1 hour 20 mins

Ingredients

500g (1lb 2oz) dried salt cod (or smoked fish) fillets, skinned and cut into pieces
3 green papayas
250g (9oz) smoked streaky bacon
3 tomatoes
3 tablespoons oil
2 onions, chopped
2 garlic cloves, peeled
1 bouquet garni
3 parsley sprigs, chopped
freshly ground black pepper

Use unripe, green papayas for this recipe, as fully ripe ones would make the dish too sweet. If you use salt cod, this will need soaking overnight to remove the excess salt. Smoked fish will not require soaking, just skinning and any remaining bones removed.

1. If using salt cod, the day before, put the pieces of fish in a large bowl of cold water. Leave them to soak for 24 hours to remove the excess salt, changing the water several times.
2. The next day, peel the papayas, remove the seeds and cut the flesh into cubes. Cut the bacon into lardons. Hull the tomatoes and roughly chop.
3. Heat the oil in a flameproof casserole over a medium heat and fry the bacon lardons and onions until golden brown, stirring them several times. Add the tomatoes and papayas, cover with cold water and simmer over a low heat for 1 hour, topping up with extra water, if necessary, so that the ingredients do not stick to the bottom of the casserole.
4. Add the fish (if using salt cod, first drain it from its soaking water), the garlic and bouquet garni. Taste, season with pepper and cook for another 10 minutes. Serve sprinkled with the chopped parsley and accompanied with rice.

Sweet Potato Cake

GÂTEAU DE PATATES DOUCES

Serves 6

Preparation time: 20 mins

Standing time: 12 hours

Cooking time: 1 hour 5 mins

Ingredients

750g (1lb 10oz) sweet potatoes

100g (3½oz) plain flour, plus extra for dusting

1 teaspoon baking powder

100g (3½oz) butter, softened, plus extra for greasing

120g (4¼oz) brown sugar

100ml (3½fl oz) unwhipped double cream

2 tablespoons aged rum (or macerated rum)

2 eggs

½ vanilla pod

2 pinches of ground cinnamon

2 pinches of freshly grated nutmeg

2 pinches of ground ginger

This cake has a deliciously soft, melt-in-the-mouth texture. Don't worry if the cake doesn't look like the photograph while it is still hot because, during baking, it will puff up but then sink down again as it cools. It needs to be left overnight to firm up.

1 Peel the sweet potatoes and cut them into dice. Cook them for 20 minutes in a saucepan of boiling water until tender, then drain thoroughly and reduce to a smooth purée in a food processor.

2 Preheat the oven to 180°C (350°F), Gas Mark 4. Sift the flour and baking powder. Beat the butter with the brown sugar in a mixing bowl or food mixer, then beat in the cream, rum and eggs. Split the vanilla pod lengthways in half and scrape out the seeds with the point of the knife into the mixture. Add the spices and then the sweet potato purée, mixing well. Finally, add the sifted flour and baking powder and fold in until smooth.

3 Grease a 25cm (10-inch) round cake tin or silicone pan with butter and dust with flour. Pour in the cake batter and bake for 45 minutes. Leave to cool a little in the tin before turning the cake out on to a wire rack and leaving it to stand until the next day.

Coconut Blancmange

COCO BLANC-MANGER

Serves 4

Preparation time: 10 mins

Chilling time: at least 3 hours

Cooking time: 3 mins

Ingredients

3 gelatine leaves

500ml (18fl oz) coconut milk

125g (4½oz) sweetened condensed milk

strips of zest from 1 unwaxed lemon

1 cinnamon stick

2 pinches of freshly grated nutmeg

To decorate

white chocolate-covered honeycomb

small thyme sprigs

Serving this simple recipe in individual dishes or glasses decorated with chocolate-covered honeycomb and tiny sprigs of thyme turns it into a stylish dessert for when you have family or friends to entertain.

1. Soak the gelatine leaves in a bowl of cold water for 5 minutes until softened.

2. Bring the coconut milk and condensed milk to the boil in a saucepan with the lemon zest and spices. Remove from the heat and leave to infuse for 5 minutes. Remove the lemon zest and cinnamon stick. Squeeze out the gelatine leaves, add to the milk mixture and stir until the gelatine has melted.

3. Pour the mixture into 4 serving dishes or glasses and leave to set in the refrigerator for at least 3 hours.

4. Serve decorated with chocolate-covered honeycomb and small thyme sprigs.

Coconut Sorbet

SORBET COCO

Serves 6–8

Preparation time: 30 mins

Infusing time: 15 mins

Chiling time: 10–15 mins

Softening time: 30 mins (if serving from the freezer)

Ingredients

1 coconut

1 litre (1¾ pints) semi-skimmed milk

1 vanilla pod

100g (3½oz) sugar

1 unwaxed lime, plus extra finely grated zest to decorate

pinch of freshly grated nutmeg

a little ground cinnamon

2 drops bitter almond extract

A fun way to serve this sorbet is to pile scoops of it into the hollowed-out shell of a fresh coconut.

1 Crack the coconut, pour the water inside it into a container (use for another recipe or serve as a drink) and remove all the flesh from the shell. Cut away the brown skin with a sharp knife and grate the flesh as finely as possible into a large bowl.

2 Heat the milk in a saucepan, slit the vanilla pod lengthways in half and scrape the seeds out with the point of the knife into the milk, then add the pod. Pour the hot milk over the grated coconut, mix well and leave to infuse for about 15 minutes. Line a sieve placed over a mixing bowl with muslin and strain the mixture through it, pressing down on the coconut with the back of a spoon to extract as much juice from the pulp as possible.

3 Add the sugar to the coconut milk and stir in. Grate in the zest from the lime, add the nutmeg, cinnamon and bitter almond extract and mix everything together.

4 Pour the mixture into an ice-cream maker and, following the manufacturer's instructions, churn for about 10–15 minutes until frozen. If not serving straight away, transfer the sorbet to a plastic container, cover with a lid and store in the freezer. Remove it from the freezer and transfer to the refrigerator about 30 minutes before serving so that it has time to soften a little and is not too hard to scoop. Serve the sorbet in scoops with a little finely grated lime zest sprinkled on top.

Tip

The sugar in this sorbet recipe can be replaced with 100ml (3½fl oz) sweetened condensed milk. If fresh coconuts are not available, you can make the sorbet with dried coconut flesh but infuse it in the hot milk for 30 minutes.

Index of Recipes

IN ALPHABETICAL ORDER

M

N

O

P

Q

R

S

T

V

Z

Index of Recipes

BY INGREDIENT

D

E

F

G

H

J

K

L

M

O

P

R

S

T

V

W

Z

Picture Credits

Illustrations

Copyright © Shutterstock

Photography

Copyright © Larousse : Martin Balme (styled by Lucie Dauchy) : p.87, 91, 97, 99, 103, 105, 111, 113, 115, 197, 201, 205, 209, 211, 217, 219, 221, 225, 227 ; Fabrice Besse (styled by Audrey Cosson) : p.231, (styled by Sabine Paris) : p.167 ; Nathalie Carnet : p.193 ; Emanuela Cino (styled by Anne Loiseau) : p.119, 121, 123, 127, 133, 137, 143, 147, 149, 151, 153, 155 ; Guillaume Czerw (styled by Sophie Dupuis-Gaulier) : p.21, 177, 187, 195, 255, 331, (styled by Alexia Janny) : p.35, 65 ; Sophie Dumont (styled by Delphine Lebrun) : p.29, 33, 45, 55, 75, 83, 85, 89, 101, 131, 135, 171, 281, 291, 315, 319 ; Caroline Faccioli (styled by Corinne Jausserand) : p.325, (styled by Sabine Paris) : p.271, 273 ; Amandine Honegger (styled by Sylvie Rost) : p.265 ; Isabelle Kanako : pp.10–13, 68–71, 92–95, 138–141, 158–161, 212–215, 238–241, 294–297, 308–311 ; Françoise Nicol (styled by Manuella Chantepie) : p.317 ; Olivier Ploton (styled by Bérengère Abraham) : p.79, 337, (styled by Blandine Boyer) : p.259, 269, 275, 279, 293, 299, 301, 303, 305, (styled by Anne Loiseau) : p.263, (styled by Catherine Moreau) : p.169, 173, 181, 183, 185, 189, 235, 243, 245, 247, 253, 257, (styled by Valérie Vermeeren) : p.175, 237 ; Aline Princet (styled by Pauline Dubois-Platet) : p.27, 251, (styled by Isabelle Guerre) : p.73 ; Franck Schmitt : p.49, 53, 57, 59, 63, 67 ; Laetitia Vasseur : p.9, 15, 17, 19, 23, 31, 37, 39, 41, 327, 329, 341 ; Pierre-Louis Viel (styled by Valéry Drouet) : p.163, 277, 289, 323.

Copyright © Shutterstock : 4–5, 6–7, 24–25, 51, 61, 125, 207, 260–261, 320–321, 332–333, 339.

UK/US terms

UK	US
aniseed	anise
aubergine	eggplant
back bacon	Canadian bacon
baking beans	pie weights
baking paper	parchment paper
baking sheet	cookie sheet
barbecue	grill
beef shin	beef shank
bird's-eye chilli	Thai chili
biscuit	cookie
black pudding	blood sausage
broad beans	fava beans
caster sugar	superfine sugar
celeriac	celery root
chicory	Belgian endive
chips	French fries
cider	hard cider
clingfilm	plastic wrap
coriander (fresh)	cilantro
cornflour	cornstarch
courgette	zucchini
crossways	crosswise
dark brown soft or dark muscovado sugar	dark brown sugar
double cream	heavy cream
egg (assumed medium unless otherwise specified)	US large egg
large egg	US extra-large egg
fast-action dried yeast	quick/rapid-rise instant yeast

UK	US
fillet steak	beef tenderloin
flank steak	skirt steak
frying pan	skillet
gammon	fresh ham
gherkins	pickles
greaseproof paper	wax paper
green/red peppers	green/red bell peppers
grill (n.)/grill (v.)	broiler/broil
groundnut oil	peanut oil
haricot beans	navy beans
hob	stove
icing sugar	confectioners' sugar
jam	jelly
Jerusalem artichoke	sunchoke
kitchen paper	paper towels
kitchen string	kitchen twine
knob of butter	pat of butter
lengthways	lengthwise
light brown soft or light muscovado sugar	light brown sugar
muslin	cheesecloth
offal	organ meats
passata	strained tomatoes
pastry	pie dough
pastry case	pie shell
pig's trotters	pigs' feet
piping bag	pastry bag
piping nozzle	piping tip
plain flour	all-purpose flour

UK	US
plaited	braided
prawns	shrimp
rasher	slice
runner beans	string beans
salad leaves	salad greens
semi-skimmed milk	2% milk
sieve	strainer
single cream	light cream
sirloin steak	short loin or porterhouse steak
sorbet	sherbet
spring onions	scallions
stalk	stem
starter	appetizer
stones	pits
streaky bacon	bacon/side bacon
swede	rutabaga
sweets	candy
tea towel	kitchen/dish towel
tin	pan
tomato purée	tomato paste
unwaxed lemon/lime	organic lemon/lime; or soak citrus fruit in a bowl of very hot water for a few minutes, then drain, scrub with a clean stiff brush and dry with paper towels
vanilla pod	vanilla bean
white kidney beans	cannellini beans
wholemeal	whole wheat

First published in Great Britain in 2025 by Hamlyn,
an imprint of Octopus Publishing Group Ltd, Carmelite House,
50 Victoria Embankment, London EC4Y 0DZ
www.octopusbooks.co.uk
www.octopusbooksusa.com

An Hachette UK Company
www.hachette.co.uk

The authorized representative in the EEA is Hachette Ireland, 8 Castlecourt Centre, Dublin 15, D15 XTP3, Ireland (email: info@hbgi.ie)

Originally published in France as *Le Petit Larousse de la Cuisine Française* by Larousse in 2023

Distributed in the US by Hachette Book Group, 1290 Avenue of the Americas, 4th and 5th Floors, New York, NY 10104

Distributed in Canada by Canadian Manda Group, 664 Annette Street, Toronto, Ontario, Canada M6S 2C8

ISBN 978-0-600-63858-2

A CIP catalogue record for this book is available from the British Library.

Printed and bound in China.

1 3 5 7 9 10 8 6 4 2

English edition 2025
Publisher: Kate Fox
Editorial Director : Natalie Bradley
Art Director: Juliette Norsworthy
Senior Editor: Leanne Bryan
Translation from the French: JMS Books LLP, Wendy Sweetser
Copyeditor: Jo Richardson
Designer: Jeremy Tilston
Production Manager: Caroline Alberti

Cover illustration: Juliette Norsworthy

Cookery notes
Standard level spoon measurements are used in all recipes.
1 tablespoon = one 15ml spoon
1 teaspoon = one 5ml spoon

Both imperial and metric measurements have been given in all recipes. Use one set of measurements only and not a mixture of both.

Eggs should be medium unless otherwise stated.